3 Days in Rhodes Travel

Welcome to Rhodes and the enchanting Dodecanese Islands—a captivating blend of history, culture, and natural beauty nestled in the sun-kissed waters of the Aegean Sea. In this travel guide, we will help you uncover the many treasures this remarkable region has to offer, providing you with a wealth of information, tips, and recommendations to ensure an unforgettable journey.

Rhodes, the largest of the Dodecanese Islands, is a true gem that effortlessly weaves together the ancient and the modern. Walk through the winding streets of the UNESCO-listed Old Town, marvel at the magnificent medieval architecture, and learn about the island's storied past. Beyond the history, discover the island's stunning beaches, charming villages, and vibrant nightlife.

But Rhodes is just the beginning. Venture to the nearby islands of Kos, Symi, Halki, and Marmaris to experience their unique charm and character. Each island offers its own distinct flavor of the Dodecanese, from the lively atmosphere of Kos to the serene beauty of Halki.

In this guide, we will take you on a comprehensive tour of the region, covering everything from must-see attractions and hidden gems to local customs and practical tips. Whether you're a history enthusiast, a beach lover, or a foodie, this corner of the Mediterranean has something to offer you. So, pack your bags and get ready to embark on an unforgettable adventure through the captivating world of Rhodes and the Dodecanese Islands.

Contents

Introduction to Rhodes Island

1.1. Overview of Rhodes Island

Welcome to Rhodes Island, a stunning sun-soaked gem situated in the southeastern Aegean Sea. As the largest of the Dodecanese islands, Rhodes is a popular holiday destination, drawing visitors from around the world with its fascinating history, beautiful beaches, and vibrant culture.

Rhodes Island is known as the "Island of the Knights" due to its rich historical connection with the Knights of Saint John, who left behind an impressive medieval legacy. The island's capital, **Rhodes City**, is divided into two distinct parts: the enchanting **Old Town**, a UNESCO World Heritage Site, and the lively **New Town**.

Rhodes offers a perfect blend of relaxation and adventure, with an extensive coastline adorned with picturesque beaches, crystal-clear waters, and hidden coves. Nature lovers will be thrilled by the lush green landscapes, while history buffs can explore ancient ruins, castles, and archaeological sites scattered across the island.

Beyond its natural beauty and historical significance, Rhodes is also famous for its mouthwatering cuisine, which combines traditional Greek flavors with Mediterranean influences. You'll find a variety of dining options, from quaint tavernas to upscale restaurants, serving delectable dishes to satisfy every palate.

In this travel guide, we'll take you on a journey through the best of Rhodes Island, offering insider tips and useful information to help you make the most of your visit. So, let's dive in and discover the wonders of Rhodes Island together!

1.2. Brief History

Rhodes Island has a rich and captivating history that spans over millennia, with its strategic location in the Aegean Sea playing a key role in the island's development. This alluring island has been shaped by the many civilizations that have occupied it over time, creating a unique cultural tapestry that endures to this day.

Prehistoric and Ancient Rhodes

The history of Rhodes Island can be traced back to the **Neolithic period**, around 5000 BCE, when the island was first inhabited by settlers. Rhodes's strategic location at the crossroads of the Mediterranean made it an attractive destination for various civilizations, including the **Minoans**, the **Mycenaeans**, and the **Dorians**.

During the **Classical period**, Rhodes Island flourished as a powerful maritime and commercial hub, with the establishment of the cities of **Ialysos**, **Lindos**, and **Kamiros**. In 408 BCE, these three cities merged to create the city of Rhodes, which became the island's new capital. The city was designed by the architect **Hippodamus** using a grid system, which was considered innovative for the time.

Rhodes Island reached its peak during the **Hellenistic period** when it was a prominent cultural and intellectual center. The island's most iconic symbol, the **Colossus of Rhodes**, a statue of the sun god Helios, was erected during this period. This awe-inspiring monument, standing about 33 meters tall, was one of the **Seven Wonders of the Ancient World**. Unfortunately, the Colossus was destroyed by an earthquake in 226 BCE, and its remains were eventually sold off by invading forces.

Roman and Byzantine Rule

In 164 BCE, Rhodes became part of the **Roman Empire**, and although the island continued to prosper as a center of trade, its cultural and political influence began to wane. Under Roman rule, Rhodes was known for its schools of philosophy, rhetoric, and sculpture, drawing scholars from all over the Mediterranean.

When the **Roman Empire split** in the 4th century CE, Rhodes Island came under the control of the **Byzantine Empire**. During this time, the island's importance declined as it faced numerous attacks from pirates and invaders. However, the Byzantines fortified the island by constructing a series of castles and fortifications, some of which still stand today.

Knights Hospitaller and the Medieval Era

In 1309, the **Knights Hospitaller**, a Christian military order, captured Rhodes Island and established their headquarters on the island. The Knights, also known as the **Knights of Saint John**, transformed

Rhodes into a formidable fortified city and a bastion of Christendom in the Eastern Mediterranean. The medieval city of Rhodes, which remains well-preserved today, was constructed during their rule, featuring impressive fortifications, palaces, and churches.

The Knights of Saint John successfully defended Rhodes against multiple sieges, most notably against the forces of the **Ottoman Empire**. However, in 1522, after a grueling six-month siege led by **Sultan Suleiman the Magnificent**, the Knights were forced to surrender and leave the island.

Ottoman Rule and Italian Occupation

Under **Ottoman rule**, which lasted until the early 20th century, Rhodes Island experienced a period of relative peace and stability, although its cultural and economic prominence continued to decline. The island became home to a diverse population of Greeks, Turks, and Jews, creating a vibrant multicultural society.

In 1912, during the **Italo-Turkish War**, Rhodes Island was occupied by **Italian forces**. The Italian occupation brought significant changes to the island, with a focus on modernization and infrastructure development. The Italians restored many of the island's historical sites, including the **Palace of the Grand Master** and the medieval city of Rhodes. They also constructed several new buildings in the Italian architectural style, such as the **Governor's Palace** and the **Aquarium**.

During World War II, Rhodes Island was briefly occupied by the **Germans** before being taken over by the **British**. The island's Jewish population, which had thrived for centuries, was decimated during the Holocaust, leaving a lasting scar on the island's history and culture.

Modern Rhodes and Greek Sovereignty

In 1947, following the end of World War II, Rhodes Island was reunited with **Greece** as part of the **Dodecanese**. Since then, the island has undergone rapid development and has emerged as one of Greece's most popular tourist destinations. Today, Rhodes Island is celebrated for its fascinating history, stunning landscapes, and vibrant culture, attracting visitors from around the world.

As you explore Rhodes Island, you'll find that its rich history is beautifully intertwined with its modern identity. The island's architectural treasures, such as the well-preserved medieval city of Rhodes, the ancient acropolis of Lindos, and the remnants of its Hellenistic past, stand as proud testaments to its storied past. At the same time, the bustling streets of Rhodes City's New Town, lively resorts, and vibrant nightlife showcase the island's modern charm.

Throughout its long and captivating history, Rhodes Island has been shaped by the many civilizations that have called it home. The island's unique blend of ancient and modern, along with its enduring spirit, make it a truly unforgettable destination for travelers seeking an authentic and memorable experience.

As you embark on your journey through Rhodes Island, we hope this brief overview of its history has provided you with a greater appreciation for the island's remarkable past and the people who have shaped it. So, take your time to wander through the ancient ruins, stroll along the cobblestone streets of the Old Town, and immerse yourself in the island's enchanting atmosphere. By doing so, you'll not only discover the beauty of Rhodes Island but also connect with the rich tapestry of its history.

1.3. Climate and Best Time to Visit

Rhodes Island enjoys a typical Mediterranean climate, characterized by hot, sunny summers and mild, wet winters. The island's idyllic weather and abundant sunshine make it an attractive destination throughout the year, but some seasons are better suited for certain activities and preferences. Here's a breakdown of Rhodes Island's climate and the best times to visit for various interests.

Spring (March to May)

Spring is a delightful time to visit Rhodes Island, as the weather is pleasant and the landscape is in full bloom. During this season, temperatures range from **16°C (61°F)** to **23°C (73°F)**, offering a comfortable climate for sightseeing and outdoor activities. The crowds are generally thinner during spring, making it an ideal time for those who prefer a more tranquil experience. As you explore the island, you'll be greeted by colorful wildflowers, lush greenery, and picturesque landscapes. This is also a great time to visit if you're interested in attending local cultural events, such as Greek Easter celebrations and the Rhodes International Film Festival.

Summer (June to August)

Summer is the peak tourist season in Rhodes Island, with temperatures ranging from **27°C (81°F)** to **31°C (88°F)**. The hot and sunny weather makes this the perfect time for beach lovers and water sports enthusiasts. The sea temperature during the summer months is warm and inviting, usually around **24°C (75°F)** to **26°C (79°F)**, making it ideal for swimming, snorkeling, and diving.

As this is the most popular time to visit, the island can get quite crowded, and accommodations may be more expensive. However, if you don't mind the bustling atmosphere and higher prices, summer offers a vibrant nightlife and numerous events and festivals, such as the Medieval Rose Festival and the Rhodes Music Festival.

Autumn (September to November)

Autumn is another excellent time to visit Rhodes Island, with temperatures ranging from **21°C (70°F)** to **28°C (82°F)**. The weather remains warm and sunny, but the intense heat of the summer months begins to subside. This makes it a perfect time for sightseeing, hiking, and enjoying the beautiful beaches without the summer crowds.

During autumn, the island takes on a more relaxed atmosphere as the tourist season starts to wind down. This is an ideal time for those looking for a quieter holiday experience, while still enjoying warm weather and plenty of sunshine. Autumn also brings the Rhodes International Street Theatre Festival, which offers a unique cultural experience.

Winter (December to February)

Winter in Rhodes Island is mild and wet, with temperatures ranging from **10°C (50°F)** to **16°C (61°F)**. While this is the least popular time to visit, it can be an attractive option for those looking to escape colder climates and enjoy a more peaceful atmosphere. The island is much quieter during the winter months, allowing visitors to explore its historical sites and charming villages without the crowds.

Rainfall is more frequent during this season, so be prepared for occasional showers and cooler temperatures. However, there are still plenty of sunny days to enjoy outdoor activities, such as hiking and exploring the island's natural beauty. Winter is also a great time to immerse yourself in local traditions and experience Christmas and New Year's Eve celebrations, Greek style.

In conclusion, the best time to visit Rhodes Island depends on your preferences and interests. Spring and autumn offer pleasant weather, fewer crowds, and a more relaxed atmosphere, making them ideal for sightseeing and outdoor activities. Summer is perfect for beachgoers and those looking for a lively holiday experience, while winter provides a quieter and more intimate setting for those seeking a peaceful getaway. No matter when you choose to visit, Rhodes Island's captivating charm and beauty are sure to create unforgettable memories.

1.4. Getting to Rhodes Island

Located in the southeastern Aegean Sea, Rhodes Island is easily accessible by various modes of transportation, making it a convenient destination for travelers. Whether you prefer to travel by air or sea, there are several options to choose from to reach this enchanting island.

By Air

Rhodes Island is served by the **Rhodes International Airport "Diagoras" (RHO)**, which is situated approximately 14 km southwest of Rhodes City. The airport receives both domestic and international flights, connecting the island with numerous destinations across Europe and beyond.

During the peak tourist season (June to August), many airlines operate direct flights to Rhodes from major European cities. Outside of the peak season, you may need to take a connecting flight through Athens or another hub. Domestic flights are available year-round, with frequent connections to and from Athens, Thessaloniki, and other Greek destinations.

Daily direct flights from the *Athens International Airport 'Eleftherios Venizelos'* to Rhodes –the flight duration is 60'. Charter flights from many European cities operate, especially during the high season

(April-October). Check a flight booking website, like Skyscanner to find prices and timetables, as they vary a lot depending on the period of the year.

Upon arrival at Rhodes International Airport, there are several transportation options to reach your accommodation, including taxis, car rentals, and public buses.

By Sea

Rhodes Island is well-connected to mainland Greece and other islands in the Aegean Sea by an extensive network of ferries and catamarans. The island has two primary ports: the **Commercial Port** in Rhodes City and the **Tourist Port** in Mandraki Harbor.

The most common sea route to Rhodes is from **Piraeus**, the main port of Athens. The journey takes approximately 12-17 hours, depending on the type of ferry and stops along the way. Ferries from Piraeus to Rhodes typically run daily during the summer months and less frequently during the off-peak season. The trip cost starts at 50€ for economy class travel and goes up to 200€ for a cabin. Before your trip check for timetables and prices here

If you are in Athens and want to go to Piraeus, you can use the metro line 1 (green line) which crosses the city of Athens, and you should stop at the final destination. If you arrive at Athens airport, take the X96 Bus. It departs every 20' from the airport bus station, and it takes about 70' to reach the port. There is also a suburban train. If you take a taxi from the airport to the harbor, it would cost you about 35 euros. Otherwise, you can get a taxi from any other part of Athens which would cost you about 15-20 euros.

In addition to the Athens-Rhodes route, there are also regular connections to and from other nearby islands, such as Kos, Symi, Patmos, and Kalymnos. This makes Rhodes an excellent base for island-hopping adventures in the Dodecanese.

During the summer months, high-speed catamarans and hydrofoils also operate between Rhodes and various other Greek islands, as well as select ports in Turkey, such as Marmaris and Fethiye. These high-speed vessels provide a faster, albeit more expensive, alternative to traditional ferries.

To book ferry tickets, you can either use online booking platforms (www.ferryhopper.gr is a popular one), contact a local travel agency, or purchase tickets directly at the port. Keep in mind that during the peak season, ferries can fill up quickly, so it's advisable to book your tickets in advance.

Whether you choose to travel by air or sea, Rhodes Island offers a range of convenient transportation options, ensuring a smooth and hassle-free journey to this beautiful and historic destination.

1.5 Arriving at Rhodes - Tips on the airport of Rhodes (RHO)

The Rhodes Airport, with the code (RHO), was recently acquired by the German company Fraport, reflecting its significance as a popular travel destination. Although it is an island airport, it is larger than one might expect, catering to a considerable number of visitors. The official website for the airport is https://www.rho-airport.gr/en.

The arrival area is in need of renovation, but the departure hall is in much better condition. As for car rentals, you can find the parking area for rental cars outside the departure area. The rental car desks are conveniently located at the exit of the arrivals area.

Rhodes Airport is approximately 25 minutes from Rhodes town, making it a convenient hub for travelers exploring the beautiful island.

The road from the airport of Rhodes to the Rhodes main town – The road network around the island is similar.

The journey from Rhodes Airport to the town is on a paved road. Although the landscape along this route may not be as captivating as the island's renowned beauty, rest assured that the charm of Rhodes will become apparent once you reach the historic Old Town.

Arriving at the airport of Rhodes with Volotea. Even though the airplane stops close to the entrance of the airport, you will have to use the shuttle and you cannot walk to the airport.

The shuttle taking you from the airplane to the airport of Rhodes The airport of Diagoras in Rhodes.

Another view of the "Diagoras Airport" in Rhodes

The area of the arrivals needs renovation. This is the baggage claim area.

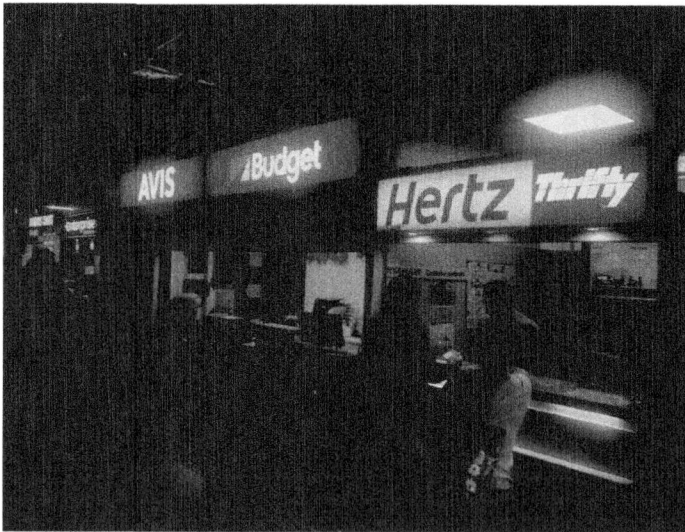

The rental car desks (Avis, Budget, Hertz, Thrifty etc) can be found when you exit the arrivals area.

A view of the area of the rent-a-car offices;

A view outside of the airport of Rhodes

To locate the parking area for the rental car offices, simply exit the arrivals area and walk about 150 meters to your left. You'll find the parking area on your right as you proceed. It is situated just outside the first door of the departures area.

The rent-a-car area is 150 meters away from the exit of the Rhodes Airport

If you leave early in the morning you can leave your car on the parking and throw the key in a special box designated by your rental car company. The desks open at six in the morning.

The departures area. Check-in area.

The duty free area has typical products to buy plus greek gourmet delicacies.

Waiting area for the buses to get you to the departures airplanes.

Transportation in Rhodes Island

Getting around Rhodes Island is relatively easy and hassle-free, thanks to its well-developed transportation infrastructure. From public transportation options like buses and taxis to private car rentals, there are plenty of ways to explore the island at your own pace.

2.1. Public Transportation

Public transportation in Rhodes Island primarily consists of buses and taxis. These options offer convenient and affordable ways to travel between the island's popular attractions, towns, and beaches.

2.1.1. Buses

The island's bus network, operated by **RODA (Rhodes Public Bus Services)**, provides extensive coverage across Rhodes Island. Buses connect Rhodes City with various towns, villages, and beaches, making them an efficient and budget-friendly mode of transportation.

The central bus station in Rhodes City, located near the New Market, serves as the primary hub for intercity and local bus routes. Bus schedules can vary depending on the season, with more frequent services during the peak tourist season (June to August). Timetables and ticket prices are available at the bus station, as well as on the RODA website.

Local buses within Rhodes City also operate on several routes, connecting the Old Town, New Town, and popular tourist spots. These buses typically run more frequently, making it easy to explore the city without a car.

Bus stops are signed. If you want to board a bus, it is better to make a hand signal to the driver. Buses are often late, and there are no timetables at the bus stops. It is common in many places to have more than one bus stop, but not every bus stops at every stop. So, it is better to ask somebody to make sure that you wait at the right stop.

Bus timetables can be found here.

When using the island's bus services, keep in mind that buses can sometimes be crowded during the peak season. Additionally, some remote areas may have limited or no bus service, so it's essential to plan your itinerary accordingly.

2.1.2. Taxis

Taxis are readily available in Rhodes City, as well as at the airport, major hotels, and popular tourist areas. You can either hail a taxi on the street, order one by phone, or use a taxi booking app.

Taxis in Rhodes Island are metered, and fares are regulated by the local government. Rates can vary depending on the time of day, distance traveled, and any additional charges for luggage or waiting time. It's a good idea to ask for an estimated fare before starting your journey to avoid any surprises.

Taxi vehicles are dark blue with white roofs.

RADIO TAXI tel. The number in Rhodes Town is **22410 69800** and outside Rhodes Town is **22410 69600.**

The standard surcharge is 3.69 euros.

Surcharges for TAXI: Starting of Taximeters 1.29 euros. Telephone calls 2.14 euros. From the Port 1.17 euros. From and to the Airport 2.83 euros. Baggage Weighting over 10 Kg. 0.43 euros. Waiting Fare per Hour 11.81 euros. Inside perimeter zone / km 0.74 euros. Outside perimeter zone / km 1.29 euros. Double Fare is charged between 00:00-05.00 Hrs. (Km /1. 29 euros). For making an appointment 6.15 euros. Dirty (Vomiting) 50.00 euros.

Extensive price list can be found here, and here You can find an updated list at the tourist office, once you arrive at the island.

Taxi prices in Rhodes Island

Here is a catalog with an approximation of what will you pay to a taxi for a transfer to different areas of the island, starting from the town of Rhodes.

Taxi Prices from the center of Rhodes town to Popular Sights and Beaches

- Rhodes to Lindos taxi price: 65 euros (one way, up to 4 persons)
- Rhodes to Tsambika beach taxi price: 40 euros
- Rhodes to Faliraki: 20 euros
- Rhodes to Kallithea Mare: 10 euros
- Rhodes to Anthony Quinn bay: 24 euros

2.2. Renting a Vehicle

For those who prefer the freedom and flexibility of exploring Rhodes Island at their own pace, renting a vehicle is an excellent option. From cars to scooters and motorbikes, there are various types of vehicles available for rent, allowing you to discover the island's hidden gems and off-the-beaten-path destinations.

2.2.1. Cars

Car rental agencies can be found in Rhodes City, at the airport, and in other major tourist areas. Numerous local and international companies offer a wide selection of vehicles to suit different needs and budgets, ranging from compact economy cars to spacious family vehicles and luxury models.

Renting a car in Rhodes Island typically requires a valid driver's license, a minimum age of 21 (or 23 for some rental agencies), and a credit card for the deposit. It's important to note that most rental cars in Greece come with manual transmissions, so if you require an automatic vehicle, be sure to specify this when making your reservation.

Driving in Rhodes Island is relatively easy, with well-maintained roads and clear signage. However, be prepared for some narrow and winding streets, particularly in the Old Town and smaller villages. Additionally, parking in Rhodes City and popular tourist areas can be limited during the peak season, so plan accordingly.

2.2.2. Scooters and Motorbikes

Scooters and motorbikes are a popular mode of transportation for visitors who want to explore Rhodes Island with a sense of adventure. They offer a convenient and fun way to navigate the island's winding roads and narrow streets while enjoying the beautiful scenery and fresh air.

Numerous rental agencies across the island offer scooters and motorbikes for rent, with various engine sizes and models to choose from. To rent a scooter or motorbike, you'll need a valid driver's license and, in some cases, a minimum age requirement (usually 18 or 21 years old). Be aware that some rental agencies may require an international driver's license or a specific motorbike license for larger engine sizes.

Start your daytrips with your rented car or motorbike with a full gas tank, because it is sometimes difficult to find a gas station. Pay attention to finding a nice parking area. The recommended hotels in this guide all provide private parking areas.

When renting a scooter or motorbike, it's crucial to prioritize safety. Always wear a helmet, follow local traffic laws, and be cautious when navigating unfamiliar roads. Keep in mind that traffic conditions can be challenging, especially in busy tourist areas and during the peak season.

2.3. Walking and Cycling

For those who enjoy a more active and eco-friendly way of exploring Rhodes Island, walking and cycling are excellent options. With its picturesque landscapes, charming villages, and historical sites, the island offers countless opportunities for memorable walks and bike rides.

Walking

Walking is not only a healthy and enjoyable way to discover Rhodes Island, but it also allows you to fully appreciate the island's rich history, architecture, and natural beauty. The medieval city of Rhodes, a UNESCO World Heritage site, is a must-visit destination for walking enthusiasts. Its narrow, cobblestone streets, historic monuments, and well-preserved city walls are best explored on foot, allowing you to immerse yourself in the atmosphere of this ancient city.

In addition to urban walks, Rhodes Island also boasts a variety of scenic hiking trails that meander through lush forests, olive groves, and along the island's stunning coastline. Popular hiking destinations include the Valley of the Butterflies, the Seven Springs (Epta Piges), and the ancient city of Kamiros. Be sure to wear comfortable shoes, carry water, and apply sunscreen when embarking on a walking adventure in Rhodes.

Cycling

Cycling is another popular way to explore Rhodes Island, offering an invigorating and environmentally friendly mode of transportation. The island's diverse terrain, ranging from flat coastal areas to hilly inland regions, caters to cyclists of all levels and abilities.

Several bike rental shops across the island offer a variety of bicycles for rent, including mountain bikes, road bikes, and e-bikes. Some rental agencies also provide helmets, locks, and other accessories to ensure a safe and enjoyable cycling experience.

Rhodes Island features numerous cycling routes that showcase the island's stunning scenery and cultural attractions. Popular routes include the coastal ride from Rhodes City to Faliraki, the picturesque journey through the villages of Koskinou and Kalithies, and the challenging ascent to the Monastery of Tsambika.

When cycling in Rhodes Island, it's essential to follow local traffic laws, wear a helmet, and stay alert to your surroundings. Be cautious when sharing the road with motor vehicles, especially on narrow and winding roads.

2.4 How to Get from the Airport to the Center of Rhodes

Rhodes International airport "Diagoras" is located near Paradisi, 15 km west of the town center. There are three ways to get to the city center, after you landing at the airport.

1. **Get a Taxi:** You can pick up a taxi at the taxi station which is located near the arrival's terminal. The trip to the town lasts 25-30' depending on the traffic, and it will cost you 25 euros. You should consider pre-booking a taxi, to avoid waiting in a long queue.
2. **Get a Bus.** There is a frequent bus service connecting the airport with the town of Rhodes. The bus station is located about 300m on your left as you exit the terminal from door 1. The trip lasts 40 minutes and it will cost you 2.20 euros. Check transportation in Rhodes below for the bus's timetables.
3. **Rent a car.** You can find rent-a-car operators at the arrivals sector (Hertz, SIXT, AVIS and Europcar). It would be better to

pre-book your car. Driving towards the town is easy, you have just to follow the signs.

Accommodations in Rhodes Island

3.1. Hotels

- Mitsis Grand Hotel Beach Hotel - Located near the medieval city of Rhodes, this 5-star hotel offers luxury amenities and stunning sea views.
- Best Western Plaza Hotel - A comfortable 4-star hotel situated in the heart of Rhodes Town, within walking distance of key attractions.

3.2. Resorts

1. Lindos Blu - This 5-star adults-only resort in Lindos offers breathtaking views, luxury facilities, and direct access to the beach.
2. Amathus Elite Suites - Located in Ixia, this upscale resort boasts elegant suites, a private beach, and top-notch service.

3.3. Bed and Breakfasts

1. Spirit of the Knights Boutique Hotel - A charming B&B set in a restored medieval building, offering a unique and intimate experience.
2. Elakati Luxury Boutique Hotel - Located in Rhodes Town, this stylish B&B offers themed rooms and personalized service.

3.4. Vacation Rentals

1. Medieval Rose Studios - Stay in a historic house in the heart of Rhodes Old Town, with modern comforts and a cozy atmosphere.

2. Villa Lindos Kalliopi - A beautiful villa in Lindos featuring a private pool, stunning views, and easy access to the beach.

3.5. Budget Accommodations

1. Stay Hostel Apartments - A budget-friendly option in Rhodes Town with dormitory-style rooms, private apartments, and a vibrant social scene.
2. Faliraki Budget Studios - Affordable studios near Faliraki beach, offering basic facilities and a convenient location.

3.6. Luxury Options

1. Elysium Resort & Spa - A 5-star resort in Kallithea with an array of luxurious amenities, including a private beach, spa, and fine dining.

2. Rodos Park Suites & Spa - Located in Rhodes Town, this 5-star hotel offers elegant rooms, a gourmet restaurant, and a tranquil spa.

3.7 A few More Recommended Budget Places

Depending on your budget we recommend one of the following places to stay in Rhodes:

If you are on a small budget, then Via Via Hotel would be an excellent choice. Located in the center of the town -perfect location to explore the old town- and within walking distance from Elli beach. The rooms are spotless and equipped with air condition, TV, mini fridge, and kettle. The staff is very polite, friendly and helpful. Free parking is possible nearby. You will be surprised with the view from the building's rooftop!

Via Via Hotel

Address: Pythagoras 45 &Lysippou 2, Rhodes Town, **Tel.:** 2241 077027

E-mail:, **Price/night:** 66 euro/2 beds room, TripAdvisor: Link, Booking.com: Link

For a mid-budget choice, you should consider **Lydia Hotel**. It is in a superb location in the very heart of the town, just a few minutes' walk from the entrance of the Medieval town. The rooms are air-conditioned, stylishly decorated with wooden floors, clean and spacious with a beautiful view from the balcony. There are a coffee/tea maker, a sat-TV, and a mini-bar. The price also includes a delicious breakfast. The hotel's personnel are friendly and helpful. At 95 euros a night for the double-bedded room, it is strongly recommended.

Lydia Hotel: **Address:** 25th Martiou St., Rhodes Town| **Tel.:** 22410-22871| **E-mail:** lydia@otenet.gr| **Price/night:** 95 euros/double bed

TripAdvisor: Link| Booking.com: Link| Website

For those who can spend some more, the Best Western Plaza hotel should be their hotel of choice for their stay in Rhodes. Best Western Plaza Hotel is located in a very convenient area with easy access to the town's sights which are within walking distance. The rooms are quiet, comfortable and spacious. You can choose pool, city or sea view. All the rooms are air-conditioned, and they have a mini bar and a LED TV screen. The price includes plentiful buffet breakfast, and you can also choose lunch or dinner. There is a great pool bar where you can enjoy a coffee or drink, and the staff is always there to help you with everything you need. A double bedded room with breakfast will cost you 145 euros.

Best Western Plaza Hotel: Address: Ierou Lohou 7, Rhodes Town| **Tel.:** 22410 22 501| **E-mail:** info@rhodesplazahotel.com| **Price/night:** 145 euros/night for the twin room

TripAdvisor: Link| Booking.com: Link| Website

Where else to stay on the island

Here are three hotels, in case you prefer to stay somewhere else than Rhodes town:

Caesar's garden hotel

Caesar's garden hotel is a peaceful place located just 10' on foot from Lindos' center. Gardens surround the hotel's buildings and from the balcony, you can see the Aegean Sea. You can book a simple room for as low as 125 euros, including breakfast or a suite with a private swimming pool, for 250-300 euros. The rooms are relaxing, comfortable and well equipped. There is not much to say, as Caesar's garden hotel is one of the top rated in the whole island.

Address: Lindos, **Tel.:** 2244 0 31537| **E-mail:** info@caesarsgardens.com| **Price/night:** 125 euros/night for the simple twin room

TripAdvisor: Link| Booking.com: Link| Website

Anelia boutique studios

Located in Faliraki, one of the most famous places among tourists, 100m from the beach and in short distance from Rhodes town (13km). Each room of the hotel has a different decoration style, and it is named after a flower. Their rooms are spacious, air-conditioned and equipped with a small dining area. The owners are very friendly and will make you feel like home!

Address: Athinas Street, Faliraki, **Tel.:** 6948587253, E-mail: cityclub@otenet.gr, **Price/night:** 90 euro/night for the twin room including breakfast

TripAdvisor: Link| Booking.com: Link| Website

Pefkos view studios

Situated in a serene location atop a hill, this lovely hotel offers breathtaking views along the Lardos-Lindos road. Surrounded by pine trees, which inspired its Greek name "Pefkos," the hotel provides a tranquil retreat. The rooms, though simply furnished, are comfortable and clean, boasting impressive views of the sea and pool from the balcony. Each room is air-conditioned and comes with a fridge and a kitchen for guests who prefer to prepare their meals. An outstanding breakfast is included in the price and served at the hotel's restaurant. The warm and hospitable staff will go above and beyond to ensure that your stay is truly enjoyable.

Address: Lardos-Lindos Road, Pefkos| **Tel.:** 22440 48379| **E-mail:** pefkosview@yahoo.gr

Price/night: 120 euro/night for the twin room including breakfast

TripAdvisor: Link| Booking.com: Link| Website

Top Attractions in Rhodes Island

4.1. Rhodes Old Town

Rhodes Old Town, a UNESCO World Heritage site, is undoubtedly one of the island's most iconic and enchanting attractions. Nestled within its impressive medieval walls, the Old Town is a labyrinth of winding cobblestone streets, magnificent palaces, and well-preserved monuments that transport visitors back in time. Here are some of the must-see attractions within Rhodes Old Town:

4.1.1. Palace of the Grand Master of the Knights

One of the most striking landmarks in the Old Town, the Palace of the Grand Master of the Knights, also known as the Kastello, once served as the headquarters of the Knights Hospitaller. This imposing fortress features stunning Gothic architecture, and today it houses a museum that showcases a collection of artifacts, mosaics, and historical exhibits. Don't miss the opportunity to explore its grand halls, beautiful courtyards, and stunning views of the harbor from the palace walls.

4.1.2. Street of the Knights

The Street of the Knights (Ippoton Street) is a well-preserved medieval thoroughfare that connects the Palace of the Grand Master with the Hospital of the Knights. Lined with impressive stone buildings, many of which served as the inns of the various "tongues" (nationalities) of the Knights Hospitaller, this cobblestone street offers a fascinating glimpse into the past. Be sure to visit the Archaeological Museum, housed in the former Hospital of the Knights, which boasts an extensive collection of ancient Greek, Roman, and Byzantine artifacts.

4.1.3. Medieval Moat and City Walls

The medieval moat and city walls of Rhodes Old Town are an engineering marvel, stretching over four kilometers and encircling the entire Old Town. The walls, constructed by the Knights Hospitaller, feature numerous towers, bastions, and gates that provided formidable defenses against invading forces. Visitors can stroll along the moat, admiring the impressive fortifications and soaking in the incredible views of the city.

4.1.4. Suleiman Mosque

Built in the 16th century by the Ottomans, the Suleiman Mosque is a beautiful example of Islamic architecture and an important historical landmark in Rhodes Old Town. Named after Sultan Suleiman the Magnificent, who led the successful siege against the Knights Hospitaller, the mosque features a spacious courtyard, a graceful minaret, and intricate decorative elements. While the mosque is not open to the public for regular visits, its exterior architecture is a must-see when exploring the Old Town.

4.1.5. Roloi Clock Tower

The Roloi Clock Tower, located near the Mosque of Suleiman, offers one of the best panoramic views of Rhodes Old Town and the surrounding area. For a small fee, visitors can climb the tower's narrow staircase to the top, where they will be rewarded with breathtaking vistas of the city, the harbor, and the coastline. The tower itself is a beautiful example of medieval architecture and an iconic symbol of the Old Town.

4.1.6. The Jewish Quarter and Kahal Shalom Synagogue

The Jewish Quarter in Rhodes Old Town, also known as La Juderia, is a testament to the island's rich multicultural history. The area, once home to a thriving Jewish community, features narrow streets, charming squares, and historic buildings. The Kahal Shalom Synagogue, built in 1577, is the oldest synagogue in Greece and serves as a museum and cultural center. The synagogue and its accompanying museum provide valuable insights into the history and culture of Rhodes's Jewish community.

4.1.2 Old Town of Rhodes: Essential Information and Tips

The Old Town of Rhodes is a significant medieval town and a UNESCO World Heritage site. Here's what you need to know before visiting:

- The town is one of the most important medieval sites worldwide.

- Around 6,000 people reside within the castle.

- Spanning 420,000 square meters, the town is incredibly vast.

- The Old Town was established in 515 BCE.

- The Palace of the Grand Master is its most notable attraction. During the Italian occupation, it served as Benito Mussolini's summer residence.

- In ancient times, the Colossus of Rhodes, one of the Seven Wonders of the Ancient World, stood here.

- Entrance to the palace costs six euros.

Tips for visiting the Old Town of Rhodes:

- Refrain from dining in the Old Town, as it is expensive and touristy. Opt for a drink or ice cream instead.

- Avoid wearing high heels, as the pebble roads can be challenging and dangerous to walk on.

- Take advantage of the shopping opportunities, including low-priced clothing, jewelry, spices, olive oil, and honey. Many shops stay open until late in the evening.

- Beware of flying red cockroaches, as the Old Town's age, proximity to the sea, and heat create ideal conditions for these insects.

- The most photographed spot is "Socrates Spring," with its picturesque towers in the background. Nearby, you can sit on beautiful stair steps for people-watching or photo-taking.

- During high season, be prepared for crowds and numerous souvenir shops. Additionally, restaurant staff may try to persuade you to dine at their establishments, which can detract from the overall experience.

Visit the UNESCO site for more information: https://whc.unesco.org/en/list/493/

Shops in the old town of Rhodes.

Eating outdoor sitting at the Old town of Rhodes.

Sitting on the stairs of this building is a popular activity at the Old Town of Rhodes.

This is a classical spot for taking some photos at the Old Town.

Fuego is a popular bar in the Old Town of Rhodes.

Walking in the Old Town.

A view of the Castle in the Old Town.

4.2. Acropolis of Lindos

The Acropolis of Lindos is another must-visit attraction on Rhodes Island, perched majestically on a clifftop overlooking the picturesque village of Lindos and its stunning bay. This archaeological site features a fascinating blend of ancient Greek, Roman, and medieval architecture, offering visitors a unique window into the island's storied past. Here are some highlights of the Acropolis of Lindos:

4.2.1. Temple of Athena Lindia

The Temple of Athena Lindia, dating back to the 4th century BCE, is the main focal point of the Acropolis. This ancient Doric temple was dedicated to the goddess Athena and was an important religious center in the Hellenistic period. Although only a few columns remain standing today, the temple's dramatic location and breathtaking views make it a memorable and awe-inspiring experience.

4.2.2. The Propylaea

As you approach the Acropolis, you'll encounter the Propylaea, a grand entranceway that once led to the Temple of Athena Lindia. This monumental gateway features a stairway flanked by columns and is reminiscent of the Propylaea found on the Athenian Acropolis. The Propylaea at Lindos is a striking example of ancient Greek architectural prowess and serves as a fitting introduction to the site.

4.2.3. The Hellenistic Stoa

The Hellenistic Stoa, a long, colonnaded structure built in the 3rd century BCE, is another noteworthy feature of the Acropolis of Lindos. The stoa once housed shops and provided a shaded area for socializing and commerce. While only a few columns remain, the stoa's picturesque location on the edge of the clifftop offers stunning views of the village and coastline below.

4.2.4. Medieval Castle of the Knights of Saint John

In addition to its ancient Greek and Roman structures, the Acropolis of Lindos also showcases the island's medieval history through the Castle of the Knights of Saint John. This fortress, constructed by the Knights Hospitaller in the 14th century, was built to protect the site and the surrounding area from pirate attacks and foreign invasions. The castle walls encompass the Acropolis, blending seamlessly with the ancient structures and providing a fascinating contrast between the different historical periods.

4.2.5. The Ancient Theatre

Situated at the foot of the Acropolis, the Ancient Theatre of Lindos is an impressive example of Greek theatrical architecture. Although partially restored, the theatre's original stone seats and stage can still be seen. The theatre was once used for performances, religious ceremonies, and public gatherings, serving as an important cultural and social hub in ancient Lindos.

To fully appreciate the Acropolis of Lindos, visitors should wear comfortable shoes, bring water, and wear sunscreen, as there is limited shade at the site. Guided tours are available, providing valuable insights into the history and significance of the various structures. The village of Lindos itself, with its whitewashed houses, narrow streets, and vibrant atmosphere, is also well worth exploring before or after your visit to the Acropolis.

In summary, the Acropolis of Lindos is a captivating attraction that showcases the rich historical tapestry of Rhodes Island. Its stunning location, diverse architectural styles, and fascinating history make it a must-see destination for any visitor to the island.

Lindos Fotos

A Panoramic view of Lindos

Lindos - another view

A closer look at the castle and the beach of Lindos

4.3. Palace of the Grand Master

The Palace of the Grand Master, also known as the Kastello or Castello, is one of the most iconic and historically significant attractions in Rhodes Island. Located within the medieval walls of Rhodes Old Town, this imposing fortress was once the residence of the Grand Master of the Knights Hospitaller and now serves as a museum and cultural center. Here are some of the key features and highlights of the Palace of the Grand Master:

4.3.1. Gothic Architecture

The Palace of the Grand Master is a stunning example of Gothic architecture, with its imposing stone walls, elaborate archways, and grand towers. As you explore the palace, you'll notice the intricate details and craftsmanship that went into its construction, showcasing the skill and artistry of the medieval builders.

4.3.2. The Grand Halls

The palace features a series of grand halls, each boasting impressive dimensions, ornate frescoes, and beautiful mosaic floors. Many of these halls were used for ceremonial purposes, hosting grand banquets and important meetings during the time of the Knights Hospitaller. Today, these halls serve as exhibition spaces, showcasing a variety of historical artifacts and artwork.

4.3.3. Palace Courtyards

The Palace of the Grand Master features several beautiful courtyards, each with its own unique charm and character. These open spaces were used for various purposes, including socializing, relaxation, and military training. The courtyards are adorned with statues, fountains, and lush greenery, providing a tranquil and picturesque setting for visitors to enjoy.

4.3.4. Palace Museum

The museum housed within the Palace of the Grand Master features a diverse collection of artifacts, spanning various periods of the island's history. Highlights of the museum include ancient Greek and Roman statues, medieval weapons and armor, religious icons, and intricate mosaics from the island of Kos. The museum offers a fascinating insight into the island's rich cultural heritage and the various civilizations that have left their mark on Rhodes.

4.3.5. Panoramic Views

One of the most memorable experiences at the Palace of the Grand Master is the stunning panoramic views of Rhodes Old Town and the harbor from the palace walls. These vistas provide a unique perspective on the city's layout and architectural beauty, as well as the surrounding landscape and coastline. Be sure to take a moment to appreciate these breathtaking views during your visit.

When visiting the Palace of the Grand Master, it's essential to wear comfortable shoes and be prepared for some stair climbing, as the fortress is spread over multiple levels. Guided tours are available, offering valuable insights into the palace's history and significance, as well as the many artifacts and exhibits on display.

In conclusion, the Palace of the Grand Master is a must-see attraction for anyone visiting Rhodes Island. Its impressive architecture, rich history, and stunning views make it a truly unforgettable experience that showcases the island's unique cultural heritage.

4.4. Ancient Kamiros

Ancient Kamiros, located on the northwest coast of Rhodes Island, is a fascinating archaeological site that showcases the remnants of one of the three ancient city-states of the island. Often referred to as the "Pompeii of Rhodes," Kamiros provides visitors with a unique glimpse into the daily life and culture of ancient Greeks who lived here centuries ago. Here are some key highlights and features of Ancient Kamiros:

4.4.1. Urban Planning and Architecture

One of the most striking aspects of Ancient Kamiros is its urban planning and architectural layout. The city was built on a series of terraces, following the natural contours of the hillside. As you wander through the site, you'll discover well-preserved examples of ancient Greek homes, public buildings, and temples, showcasing the architectural styles and building techniques of the time.

4.4.2. The Agora

The Agora, or marketplace, was the commercial and social heart of Ancient Kamiros. This large open space was surrounded by porticoes, shops, and storerooms, where merchants and traders would gather to conduct business. Today, you can still see the remains of these structures, providing a sense of the bustling activity that once took place here.

4.4.3. The Stoa and Fountain House

The Stoa, a long, colonnaded structure, is one of the most prominent features of Ancient Kamiros. The Stoa provided a shaded area for socializing and relaxation, as well as a place for merchants to display their goods. Nearby, you'll find the Fountain House, a public building that once supplied the city's inhabitants with fresh water. The remains of the Fountain House still showcase the ancient water distribution system, including a series of terracotta pipes and water basins.

4.4.4. Temples and Sanctuaries

Ancient Kamiros is home to several temples and sanctuaries dedicated to various gods and goddesses. The most significant of these is the Temple of Athena, which stands atop the highest terrace of the city. Other notable religious sites include the Sanctuary of the Dioscuri and the Sanctuary of Apollo Erethimios. These sacred spaces offer a fascinating insight into the religious practices and beliefs of the ancient inhabitants of Kamiros.

4.4.5. The Acropolis

At the highest point of Ancient Kamiros, you'll find the Acropolis, a fortified area that once housed the city's most important religious and political structures. Although only the foundations remain today, the Acropolis offers stunning views of the surrounding landscape and coastline, making it a worthwhile stop during your visit.

To make the most of your visit to Ancient Kamiros, be sure to wear comfortable shoes, bring water, and wear sunscreen, as there is limited shade at the site. Guided tours are available, providing valuable insights into the history and significance of the various structures and features of the ancient city.

In summary, Ancient Kamiros is a captivating archaeological site that allows visitors to step back in time and experience the daily life and culture of ancient Greeks who once inhabited Rhodes Island. Its well-preserved remains, picturesque setting, and fascinating history make it a must-visit destination for anyone interested in ancient history and archaeology.

4.5. Valley of the Butterflies

The Valley of the Butterflies, known as Petaloudes in Greek, is a unique and enchanting natural attraction on Rhodes Island. Located in a lush, verdant valley near the village of Theologos, this beautiful area is home to millions of Jersey Tiger Moths (Euplagia quadripunctaria) that gather here during the summer months. The combination of dense vegetation, flowing streams, and the colorful presence of these delicate creatures create a magical atmosphere that is sure to captivate visitors. Here are some highlights and features of the Valley of the Butterflies:

4.5.1. Walking Trails and Bridges

The Valley of the Butterflies features well-maintained walking trails and wooden bridges that allow visitors to explore the area and observe the moths up close. As you wander through the valley, you'll be surrounded by the soothing sounds of flowing water and the gentle rustling of leaves, creating a serene and calming environment. Be sure to tread lightly and avoid disturbing the moths as you make your way through the valley.

4.5.2. Natural Beauty and Tranquility

One of the main draws of the Valley of the Butterflies is its breathtaking natural beauty. The valley is home to a diverse array of flora, including oriental sweetgum trees, which release a distinctive resin that attracts the Jersey Tiger Moths. The combination of lush greenery, colorful flowers, and the enchanting presence of the moths creates a truly mesmerizing setting that is perfect for nature lovers and photographers alike.

4.5.3. The Museum of Natural History

At the entrance to the Valley of the Butterflies, you'll find the Museum of Natural History. This small but informative museum showcases the various species of butterflies and moths found on Rhodes Island, as well as other local flora and fauna. The museum also offers insights into the unique ecosystem of the valley and the life cycle of the Jersey Tiger Moth.

4.5.4. Monastery of Panagia Kalopetra

Perched atop a hill overlooking the Valley of the Butterflies is the Monastery of Panagia Kalopetra. This 18th-century monastery, dedicated to the Virgin Mary, offers stunning views of the valley and the surrounding landscape. Visitors are welcome to explore the monastery and its peaceful courtyard, making it a worthwhile stop during your visit to the Valley of the Butterflies.

To fully enjoy your visit to the Valley of the Butterflies, it's essential to wear comfortable shoes, bring water, and wear sunscreen, as the area can become quite warm during the summer months. Keep in mind that the Jersey Tiger Moths are a seasonal attraction, with the peak months being June to September.

In summary, the Valley of the Butterflies is a must-visit destination for nature lovers and those seeking a tranquil escape from the hustle and bustle of Rhodes Island's more popular tourist spots. Its enchanting atmosphere, vibrant natural beauty, and fascinating wildlife make it a truly unforgettable experience.

4.6. Prasonisi Peninsula

The Prasonisi Peninsula is a remarkable and picturesque destination located at the southernmost tip of Rhodes Island. This stunning area, where the Aegean Sea meets the Mediterranean Sea, is characterized by its unique sandbar and beach that connects the main island to a smaller islet. Prasonisi is a haven for water sports enthusiasts, particularly windsurfers and kitesurfers, thanks to its ideal wind conditions. Here are some highlights and features of the Prasonisi Peninsula:

4.6.1. Windsurfing and Kitesurfing Paradise

Prasonisi is renowned for its excellent wind conditions, making it a top destination for windsurfers and kitesurfers from around the world. The area benefits from consistent side-shore winds throughout the summer months, providing ideal conditions for both beginners and experienced riders. Several water sports centers on the peninsula offer equipment rentals, lessons, and storage facilities, ensuring a hassle-free experience for visitors.

4.6.2. Unique Beaches and Sandbar

The Prasonisi Peninsula is home to a unique sandbar that connects Rhodes Island to the smaller islet of Prasonisi. This natural feature creates two distinct beaches on either side of the sandbar: one with calm, shallow waters perfect for swimming and relaxing, and the other with choppier waters and waves suited for water sports. Depending on the season and tide, the sandbar may be submerged, turning Prasonisi into a separate island, or it may be exposed, allowing visitors to walk between the two landmasses.

4.6.3. Lighthouse and Panoramic Views

At the tip of the Prasonisi Peninsula, you'll find a picturesque lighthouse that stands as a sentinel over the area. The lighthouse, which dates back to the early 20th century, is a popular spot for capturing stunning photographs of the surrounding seascape. The area around the lighthouse also offers panoramic views of the coastline, the sandbar, and the sparkling waters of the Aegean and Mediterranean Seas.

4.6.4. Flora and Fauna

The Prasonisi Peninsula is home to unique flora and fauna that have adapted to the area's windswept conditions. As you explore the peninsula, you'll encounter a variety of plants, such as low shrubs, grasses, and wildflowers, that provide a rugged yet beautiful backdrop for your visit. The area is also an important habitat for several bird species, making it an interesting destination for birdwatching enthusiasts.

When visiting the Prasonisi Peninsula, be sure to bring sun protection, water, and comfortable shoes for walking on the sand and rocky terrain. There are a few seasonal facilities on the peninsula, including cafes and shops, but it's a good idea to come prepared with any essentials you may need.

4.7. Seven Springs

Seven Springs, or Epta Piges in Greek, is a beautiful and tranquil oasis located in the heart of Rhodes Island, approximately 30 kilometers from Rhodes Town. This lush, green valley is renowned for its seven natural springs, which converge to form a small lake. The cool, shaded environment, combined with the soothing sounds of flowing water, make Seven Springs an ideal destination for those seeking respite from the summer heat. Here are some highlights and features of Seven Springs:

4.7.1. Walking Trails and Picnic Areas

The Seven Springs area offers a network of walking trails that meander through the forest, allowing visitors to explore the valley and enjoy the sights and sounds of nature. The trails are well-maintained and suitable for all fitness levels, making them accessible to everyone. There are also several picnic areas scattered throughout the valley, where visitors can relax and enjoy a leisurely meal surrounded by the beauty of the forest.

4.7.2. The Lake and Waterfall

At the heart of Seven Springs is a small, crystal-clear lake, fed by the seven springs. This picturesque lake is home to a variety of fish and waterfowl, adding to the area's charm. The lake is also fed by a small waterfall, creating a serene spot to relax and enjoy the soothing sounds of water cascading over the rocks. For those feeling adventurous, you can even take a refreshing dip in the lake's cool waters.

4.7.3. The Tunnel

One of the unique features of Seven Springs is the narrow tunnel that leads to the lake. This 186-meter-long tunnel was built during the Italian occupation of Rhodes and is now a popular attraction for visitors. Walking through the tunnel can be an exhilarating experience, as you'll need to wade through shallow water in near-total darkness. Be sure to wear appropriate footwear and carry a waterproof flashlight if you decide to embark on this adventure.

4.7.4. Flora and Fauna

Seven Springs is home to a diverse range of flora and fauna, making it a paradise for nature lovers and photographers. The area's dense vegetation, including plane trees, pines, and oleanders, provides a habitat for numerous bird species, as well as small mammals and reptiles. The valley's unique microclimate also supports a variety of aquatic plants and insects, adding to the area's biodiversity.

When visiting Seven Springs, be sure to wear comfortable shoes, bring water, and wear sun protection, as some parts of the trails may be exposed to the sun. There is a small café near the entrance of the valley, where you can purchase refreshments and snacks.

Best Beaches on Rhodes Island

Enjoy the sea and the sun in these top 10 beaches in Rhodes. The beach's position can be found on the map at the end of this guide.

5.1 Agios Pavlos Beach

Distance from Rhodes City: 50 km

Agios Pavlos Beach is a hidden gem nestled on the southeastern coast of Rhodes Island, near the historic village of Lindos. This picturesque beach is split into two charming coves and features a quaint chapel at its edge, adding to its allure. Agios Pavlos is a favorite spot for locals from the upper part of Lindos, while also attracting many foreign visitors. With its mix of sand, pebbles, and crystal-clear waters, Agios Pavlos offers an idyllic setting for relaxation and recreation.

5.1.1. Getting to Agios Pavlos Beach

To reach Agios Pavlos Beach, you can either drive or take public transportation. If you're driving from Rhodes City, follow the main coastal road heading south towards Lindos. There's a parking area near the beach, but you'll need to park your car a bit further away and then walk down to the shore. The walk takes approximately 10-15 minutes and offers stunning views of the coastline.

Alternatively, you can take a bus from Rhodes City to Lindos, which typically takes around 1 hour and 15 minutes. From Lindos, it's about a 20-minute walk to Agios Pavlos Beach. You can also hire a taxi from Lindos or arrange for a boat ride from Lindos Beach to Agios Pavlos.

5.1.2. Beach Amenities and Activities

Agios Pavlos Beach caters to different preferences, with one side offering sunbeds, food, and island music for a lively atmosphere, while the other side provides a more secluded and peaceful setting for relaxation. The beach's rocky formations are perfect for diving into the refreshing waters or snorkeling to explore the vibrant marine life.

Prices for sunbed rentals vary, but expect to pay around €5-€10 for a set of two sunbeds and an umbrella. The nearby beach bars and restaurants offer a range of food and drink options, with prices varying depending on the establishment.

5.1.3. Exploring the Surroundings

While at Agios Pavlos Beach, don't miss the opportunity to visit the nearby chapel of St. Paul (Agios Pavlos), a charming white-washed building with stunning views of the sea. History and movie enthusiasts can also hire a boatman to take them to the Laki, a strait where some scenes from the classic film "The Guns of Navarone" were shot.

5.1.4. Tips for Visiting

When visiting Agios Pavlos Beach, be sure to bring sun protection, water, and comfortable shoes for walking. The beach can get quite busy during the peak summer months, so consider visiting earlier in the day or during the shoulder season for a more tranquil experience.

5.2 Agathi Beach

Distance from Rhodes City: 36Km. Features and facilities: Food, Umbrellas, and sunbeds

Agathi Beach, also known as Haraki Beach, is a stunning and tranquil spot situated on the eastern coast of Rhodes Island. This beautiful sandy beach, with its crystal-clear turquoise waters, is surrounded by imposing hills, creating a secluded and serene atmosphere. Agathi Beach is an ideal destination for families and anyone seeking a relaxing beach experience away from the bustling tourist crowds.

Fine, wet sand and some canteens - this is the only thing you will find on Agathi. It is a beautiful, sheltered, cozy beach, and the only sign of civilization are its canteens, all of them offering more or less the same food - fried eggs, English breakfast, sandwiches, burgers, salads, French fries, and souvlaki.

Camping is possible there, so take your sleeping bag and camp at the cave which is at the end of the beach. An ideal spot to spend the night.

5.2.1. Getting to Agathi Beach

To reach Agathi Beach, you can either drive or take public transportation. If you're driving from Rhodes City, follow the main coastal road heading south towards Lindos. Just after the village of Haraki, take a right turn, following the signs to Agathi Beach. There's a parking area near the beach, and from there, it's just a short walk down to the shore.

Alternatively, you can take a bus from Rhodes City to Haraki, which typically takes around 1 hour. From Haraki, it's about a 20-minute walk to Agathi Beach. Taxis are also available from Haraki, or you can arrange a boat ride from Haraki Beach to Agathi Beach.

To get to the beach, follow the signs from Haraki (10 minutes along an easy dirt road). Halfway along the road you come upon the medieval castle of Feraklos. Al canteens at the beach rent out sun beds umbrellas and have toilets and showers. There is also a card-operated telephone on the beach.

5.2.2. Beach Amenities and Activities

Agathi Beach offers a range of amenities, including sunbeds and umbrellas for rent, as well as a few beach bars and tavernas where you can enjoy refreshments and local cuisine. The calm, shallow waters make the beach particularly suitable for families with young children or those who enjoy leisurely swimming and snorkeling.

Prices for sunbed rentals are generally around €5-€10 for a set of two sunbeds and an umbrella. The nearby tavernas offer a variety of food and drink options, with prices varying depending on the establishment.

5.2.3. Exploring the Surroundings

While at Agathi Beach, consider exploring the nearby Feraklos Castle, perched on a hill overlooking the beach. This medieval fortress dates back to the Byzantine era and was later occupied by the Knights of St. John. The walk up to the castle is steep but offers rewarding panoramic views of the beach and surrounding coastline.

5.3 Antony Quinn Bay

Distance from Rhodes City: 15 km

Antony Quinn Bay is a picturesque and charming beach located on the eastern coast of Rhodes Island, just a short distance from Rhodes City. This stunning bay, with its natural stone surfaces and emerald-green waters, is surrounded by lush pine trees that reach down to the water's edge. The beach gained fame and its current name after actor Anthony Quinn purchased the land while filming "The Guns of Navarone" on the island. Today, Antony Quinn Bay is a popular destination for beach lovers, particularly among younger visitors and those seeking a unique and breathtaking beach experience.

5.3.1. Getting to Antony Quinn Bay

To reach Antony Quinn Bay, you can either drive or take public transportation. If you're driving from Rhodes City, follow the main coastal road heading south towards Faliraki. The beach is well signposted, and there's a parking area near the bay. From the parking area, it's a short walk down to the beach.

Alternatively, you can take a bus from Rhodes City to Faliraki, which typically takes around 20 minutes. From Faliraki, you can either walk for about 30 minutes or take a taxi to Antony Quinn Bay.

5.3.2. Beach Amenities and Activities

Antony Quinn Bay offers a range of amenities, including umbrellas and sunbeds for rent, as well as a canteen at the top of the rocks where you can grab food and refreshments. The beach's unique natural stone surfaces and crystal-clear waters make it ideal for sunbathing, swimming, and snorkeling.

Prices for sunbed rentals are generally around €5-€10 for a set of two sunbeds and an umbrella. The canteen offers a variety of food and drink options, with prices varying depending on the items.

5.3.3. Exploring the Surroundings

While at Antony Quinn Bay, take the time to explore the surrounding rocky landscape and enjoy the panoramic views of the bay and the coastline. The beach's central rock formation offers a limited number of sunbeds, making it a prime spot for sunbathing and taking in the breathtaking scenery.

5.3.4. Tips for Visiting

When visiting Antony Quinn Bay, keep in mind that the sharp rocks in and out of the water may not be suitable for families with small children or seniors. The beach is most popular in July and August, while the water may be too cold for swimming during other times of the year.

Be sure to bring sun protection, water, and comfortable shoes for walking. Arrive early during the peak summer months to secure a prime spot on the beach and avoid the crowds.

5.4 Tsambika Beach

Tsambika Beach, also known as Tsampika Beach, is a stunning and popular destination located on the eastern coast of Rhodes Island. This beautiful, expansive beach features fine golden sand, crystal-clear emerald waters, and an array of colorful flags marking the various eating establishments and beach sports centers. The beach takes its name from the nearby Monastery of the Virgin of Tsambika, perched on an imposing rock that overlooks the beach. The Virgin of

Tsambika is said to perform miracles, and many women pray to her for fertility assistance.

5.4.1. Getting to Tsambika Beach

To reach Tsambika Beach, you can either drive or take public transportation. If you're driving from Rhodes City, follow the main coastal road heading south towards Lindos. The beach is well signposted, and there's a parking area near the beach. From the parking area, it's a short walk down to the shore.

Alternatively, you can take a bus from Rhodes City to Tsambika Beach, which typically takes around 45 minutes. The bus stop is conveniently located near a mini-market, just a short walk from the beach.

5.4.2. Beach Amenities and Activities

Tsambika Beach offers a range of amenities, including umbrellas and sunbeds for rent, various eating establishments, beach sports centers, and a mini-market close to the bus stop. The beach's calm, clear waters make it ideal for swimming, sunbathing, and water sports such as jet-skiing, windsurfing, and paddleboarding.

Prices for sunbed rentals are generally around €5-€10 for a set of two sunbeds and an umbrella. The various eating establishments offer a variety of food and drink options, with prices varying depending on the venue.

5.4.3. Exploring the Surroundings

While at Tsambika Beach, consider visiting the nearby Monastery of the Virgin of Tsambika, which is accessible by a steep footpath leading up from the beach. The hike to the monastery takes about 30 minutes and offers spectacular panoramic views of the beach and surrounding coastline.

5.4.4. Tips for Visiting

When visiting Tsambika Beach, be sure to bring sun protection, water, and comfortable shoes for walking. The beach can get crowded during the peak summer months, so it's a good idea to arrive early to secure a prime spot on the beach.

5.5 Lindos

Distance from Rhodes City: 50Km

Features and facilities: Public Transportation, Food, Umbrellas and sunbeds, Hotels

Follow the sign for the beach, and you will find yourself at the left-hand end, while if you go straight down below the Acropolis, down Pallas St., you will find yourself at the right-hand end, known as Pallas Beach. They are two different beaches sharing the same bay. Sun beds everywhere, umbrellas, tavernas, crowds of people - from groups brought by coach from other parts of Rhodes to Brits who settle in Lindos each year for the whole summer. Old-timers reminisce about the little blue flowers that used to grow in the sand, and about the celebrity yachts which once anchored here in the beach's heyday. Now, unfortunately, the place seems to have entered a decline. If you dislike crowds, make for Pallas Beach, which is relatively quieter. The water is shallow and ideal for young children.

5.6 Traganou Beach

Traganou Beach is a charming and tranquil destination located on the eastern coast of Rhodes Island, known for its unique rocky landscape, clear turquoise waters, and picturesque sea caves. This relatively secluded beach offers a peaceful and relaxing atmosphere, making it an ideal choice for visitors seeking a more serene beach experience away from the bustling crowds.

5.6.1. Getting to Traganou Beach

To reach Traganou Beach, you can either drive or take public transportation. If you're driving from Rhodes City, follow the main coastal road heading south towards Faliraki. The beach is well signposted, and there's a parking area close to the beach.

Alternatively, you can take a bus from Rhodes City to Faliraki, which typically takes around 20 minutes. From Faliraki, you can either walk for about 40 minutes or take a taxi to Traganou Beach.

5.6.2. Beach Amenities and Activities

Traganou Beach offers a more natural and unspoiled beach experience, with fewer amenities than some of the more popular beaches on Rhodes Island. There are no sunbeds or umbrellas for rent, so visitors should bring their own beach equipment. However, the beach's unique landscape, featuring large rocks and sea caves, provides ample opportunities for exploration and relaxation.

The calm and clear waters of Traganou Beach make it an excellent spot for swimming, snorkeling, and diving. The beach's sea caves, in particular, offer a fascinating underwater world waiting to be discovered.

5.7 Afantou

Distance from Rhodes City: 18Km

Features and facilities: Public Transportation, Food, Umbrellas and sunbeds, Hotels

Families with ice-boxes and folding chairs, couples with tents, Brits with their hot dogs and beers at the canteen, young people racing their jet-skis, locals coming for fish at the local tavernas. There is ample room for them all on the vast beach at Afantou, and no one feels crowded. A sandy beach with some pebbles, and sea that deepens quite abruptly. Some sections of the beach are commercially organized while others are not. Among the foreigners, this is a favorite spot with Brits and Germans. There is a small number of small restaurants, beach sports centers, and fish tavernas. On the coast road, you will also find the Rhodes golf course.

5.8 Gennadi

Distance from Rhodes City: 63Km

Beach with blue flag. Sand and small pebbles as far as the eye can see - and the liveliest beach parties held anywhere on Rhodes. Basically a continuation of Kiotari, Gennadi combines two different characters: on the one hand there's the vast beach where there's always room for you and your friends to spread out your beach towels - only parts of the beach are commercially organized - while on the other there are the Sunday parties with guests DJ's at the new Sundance beach bar, which opened last year and has transformed the character of the beach, attracting all the hip young people from around the island. The beach is separated from the village, which lies above the main road, but along the way you will find tavernas, rooms to rent, small hotels and the villas of wealthy local people.

5.9 Haraki

Distance from Rhodes City: 36Km

Features and facilities: Public Transportation, Food, Umbrellas, and sunbeds, Hotels

The sight of children searching for shells among the pebbles, couples gazing out to sea from the balconies of their rented rooms, sun-burned mothers wheeling pushchairs up and down - this attractive little bay offers a family atmosphere. It is mainly visited by tourists renting apartments nearby, but families of local people also come out with their umbrellas and settle themselves on the no-charge section in the center of the beach. The right-hand side of the beach has large pebbles, while to the left there is sand.

If you choose to swim at the far right end of the beach, you will have a good view of the Feraklos castle. Along the promenade with the rented rooms, there are mini-markets, cafes, and a foreign press agency.

5.10 Stegna

Distance from Rhodes City: 29Km

On the right, you will find peace and quiet and a family atmosphere, while on the left a private beach for guests of the one and only hotel, occupied mainly by groups from Germany. The beach is located just 500 meters along the road from Archangelos and is the ideal bathing place for the local villagers. This makeup most of the bathers on the beach, along with the visitors staying at the hotel. An ideal location for those seeking relaxation. Sand and pebbles, a kiosk, water sports, a few tavernas and rooms for rent.

Tsampika Beach: Photos and Tips

The beach at Tsampika is sandy and pretty wide.

Tsampika beach - a view of the umbrellas area.

Umbrella Prices and Safety Box Options

The cost of renting an umbrella at the beach is €10. For an additional €5, totaling €15, you can also have a safety box included with your umbrella. The safety box is a convenient option for storing your mobile, wallet, and other valuable items when you go for a swim in the sea. If you're concerned about leaving your belongings unattended, using the safety box might be a wise choice.

Extra Costs and Amenities at Tsampika Beach

At Tsampika Beach, visitors should note that the safe boxes provided with the umbrellas come with an additional charge of €5. Iced coffees are priced at €3, fresh orange juice at €3.50, and a Greek salad costs €6.

Spanning two kilometers in length and seventy meters in width, Tsampika Beach is a popular destination known for its lively atmosphere, featuring numerous beach bars and umbrellas. Despite the crowds, with over a thousand people visiting the beach, it maintains a relaxed and quiet ambiance. Nudism is not practiced here, and the beach is well-sheltered from strong winds.

The picturesque backdrop of green mountains and the absence of hotels or houses in sight add to Tsampika Beach's allure. However, it is important to note that there is no table service at the umbrellas on the beach. Visitors will need to head to the beach bars and canteens located behind the umbrellas to order their food and drinks.

The mountains behind Tsampika beach. There is a beautiful monastery on the top which worths a visit on its own.

Tsampika beach also has a water park for kids inside the sea.

The water park at Tsampika beach

The sand at Tsampika beach.

The water is suitable for children as it is not deep.

Once you've enjoyed your time at Tsampika beach, consider dining at Perigiali seafood restaurant, located in the picturesque area of Stegna. Although Tsampika may not be as well-known as Lindos or Kallithea beaches, many visitors find it to be the best overall beach experience on the island.

Glystra Beach: A Tranquil Family Getaway

Situated just a 15-minute drive from Lindos, Glystra Beach is an ideal destination for families seeking a serene and relaxing beach experience. This sandy beach stretches approximately 350 meters in length and 20 meters in width, offering ample space for visitors to unwind and enjoy the sun.

The beach is equipped with sunbeds and umbrellas, available for rent at 12 euros for a set of two sunbeds and one umbrella. Additionally, a complimentary safety box is provided for securely storing your belongings. For refreshments, there is a canteen selling drinks and food, although the prices can be on the higher side, with iced coffee at 4 euros, orange juice at 5 euros, and a liter of water at 2 euros.

The water at Glystra Beach is pleasantly warm and remains shallow for the first ten meters, making it suitable for families with children. In contrast to the bustling beaches of Lindos or Kallithea, Glystra Beach offers a peaceful atmosphere, allowing visitors to unwind and truly appreciate the beauty of Rhodes.

Access to the beach is straightforward by car, and parking is available along the road before reaching the canteen on the beach. So, if you're seeking a quiet and relaxing beach destination on Rhodes Island, Glystra Beach is undoubtedly worth a visit.

Glystra beach is suitable for families with children. The availability of sunbeds, umbrellas, and a canteen ensures that families can spend the entire day at the beach without worrying about refreshments or food.

Glystra beach has clean waters - he shallow waters extending ten meters from the shoreline create a perfect setting for young ones to play and swim under the watchful eyes of their parents.

A view of Glystra beach

Crystal clear waters at Tsampika beach

Visitors to Glystra Beach should be aware that the on-site canteen, while convenient, tends to be quite expensive due to the lack of alternative options for food and drinks in the area. As it is the sole source of refreshments at the beach, the canteen can charge a premium for its offerings.

Travelers are advised to come prepared by bringing their own snacks, water, and other essentials, especially if they plan to spend a full day at the beach. By doing so, they can avoid the high costs of the canteen and still enjoy the beautiful surroundings and tranquil atmosphere of Glystra Beach.

You can park your car outside Glystra beach

Dining and Nightlife

6.1. Traditional Greek Cuisine

Rhodes Island is a melting pot of flavors, offering visitors an opportunity to indulge in authentic and delicious Greek cuisine. Traditional dishes are prepared with fresh, locally-sourced ingredients, and many restaurants take pride in their culinary heritage. Here are some tips and suggestions for enjoying traditional Greek cuisine on Rhodes Island:

- Seek out local tavernas: For an authentic Greek dining experience, visit local tavernas where you can savor home-cooked meals in a warm and welcoming atmosphere. These family-run establishments often have generations of culinary expertise and serve dishes made from their own family recipes.

- Must-try dishes: Don't miss out on traditional Greek dishes such as moussaka (eggplant and minced meat casserole), souvlaki (grilled meat skewers), dolmades (stuffed grape leaves), tzatziki (yogurt, cucumber, and garlic dip), and fresh seafood, including grilled octopus and fried calamari.

- Sample local specialties: Rhodes Island has its own unique culinary traditions. Be sure to taste melekouni (honey and sesame seed bars), pitaroudia (chickpea fritters), and local cheeses such as anthotyros and myzithra.

- Enjoy the Mediterranean diet: The Greek cuisine is part of the healthy Mediterranean diet, which emphasizes fresh fruits, vegetables, whole grains, and healthy fats such as olive oil. Embrace this nutritious lifestyle during your stay on Rhodes Island.

- Savor Greek wines: Greece is known for its wine production, and Rhodes is no exception. Sample local wines like Athiri, Mandilaria, and Moscato at restaurants or visit wineries for a tasting experience.

- Ouzeries and mezedopoleia: For a casual dining experience, visit ouzeries or mezedopoleia, where you can enjoy ouzo (anise-flavored liqueur) or other beverages accompanied by a variety of small dishes called meze.

Nightlife on Rhodes Island:

Rhodes Island offers a vibrant and diverse nightlife scene, catering to a range of tastes and preferences. From lively bars and clubs to sophisticated venues, there's something for everyone.

- Bar Street (Orfanidou Street) in Rhodes Town: This popular strip is lined with bars, clubs, and restaurants, offering a lively atmosphere and a variety of entertainment options.

- Lindos: Lindos boasts a more laid-back nightlife scene, with stylish rooftop bars and charming tavernas nestled in the picturesque village.

- Faliraki: Known for its energetic nightlife, Faliraki offers a wide selection of clubs, bars, and beach parties that cater to the younger crowd.

- Ialyssos and Kremasti: These coastal towns feature a mix of lively bars, beach clubs, and laid-back lounges, offering a balanced nightlife experience.

- Live music venues: Enjoy traditional Greek music and performances at various establishments throughout the island, or catch a live band or DJ at a contemporary music venue.

Remember to drink responsibly and respect local customs while enjoying the nightlife on Rhodes Island.

6.2. International Cuisine

Rhodes Island offers a diverse range of dining options, including a wide selection of international cuisine. From Italian and Asian to European and Middle Eastern flavors, there is something to satisfy every palate. Here are some tips for enjoying international cuisine on Rhodes Island:

- Italian and Mediterranean: The island has a variety of Italian and Mediterranean restaurants serving classics such as pasta, risotto, and wood-fired pizza, along with a range of seafood and grilled dishes. Look for eateries with an authentic atmosphere and a focus on fresh ingredients.

- Asian: Rhodes Island is home to several Asian restaurants, including Chinese, Japanese, and Thai options. Many of these establishments offer a fusion of flavors and contemporary twists on traditional dishes.

- European: From French and Spanish to German and British cuisine, Rhodes has a selection of eateries serving up European fare. Look for restaurants with a reputation for quality and authenticity.

- Middle Eastern: Rhodes Island's multicultural heritage is reflected in its Middle Eastern dining options, which include restaurants serving Lebanese, Turkish, and Israeli dishes. Enjoy delicious hummus, falafel, and shawarma in a vibrant and welcoming setting.

Top Recommendations:

1. Marco Polo Cafe (Italian & Mediterranean) Address: 45 Alexandrou Diakou, Rhodes Town 85100, Greece Website: https://www.marcopolocafe.gr/

2. Ronda Beach Restaurant (Italian & Mediterranean) Address: Akti Miaouli, Rhodes Town 85100, Greece Website: http://www.rondabeach.gr/

3. Noodle Box (Asian) Address: 32 Griva Street, Rhodes Town 85100, Greece Website: http://www.noodleboxrhodes.com/

4. Tamam (Middle Eastern) Address: 1 Leontos, Rhodes Town 85100, Greece Website: https://www.facebook.com/Tamam-Rhodes-173927126008591/

5. Sissitio (European) Address: 35 Pythagora, Rhodes Town 85100, Greece Website: https://www.sissitio.com/

6.3. Seafood and Coastal Delights

Being surrounded by the Mediterranean Sea, Rhodes Island is a haven for seafood lovers. With an abundance of fresh fish and seafood caught daily, the island offers a range of coastal delights to savor. Here are some tips for enjoying seafood on Rhodes Island:

- Choose fresh and local: Visit restaurants and tavernas that pride themselves on serving freshly-caught seafood. Look for dishes made with seasonal and locally-sourced ingredients.

- Popular seafood dishes: Indulge in delicious seafood dishes such as grilled octopus, fried calamari, saganaki (fried cheese with shrimp or mussels), and fish souvlaki.

- Traditional fish tavernas: For an authentic experience, dine at traditional fish tavernas, often located near the harbor or by the sea. These establishments usually offer a range of fresh fish and seafood dishes, as well as stunning views.

- Fish markets: Visit local fish markets to purchase fresh seafood and gain an insight into the island's fishing traditions. You can also find seafood eateries nearby, where you can enjoy a meal made with the freshest catch.

- Beachfront dining: Many coastal towns and villages on Rhodes Island have restaurants and tavernas right on the beach, offering a unique dining experience with breathtaking views of the sea.

Seafood and Coastal Delights:

Koozina (Seafood & Mediterranean)

Address: 20 Pindarou, Rhodes Town 85100, Greece

Website: http://www.koozinarestaurant.com/

Alexis 4 Seasons (Seafood & Greek)

Address: 18 Sofokleous, Rhodes Town 85100, Greece

Website: https://www.facebook.com/alexis4seasons/

To Kanoni (Seafood & Mediterranean)

Address: Kanoni Beach, Kallithea 85100, Greece

Website: http://www.tokanonikallithea.com/

Nikolas Taverna (Seafood & Greek)

Address: Haraki Beach, Haraki 85102, Greece

Website: https://www.facebook.com/nikolastaverna/

Perasma Taverna (Seafood & Greek)

Address: Epar.Od. Faliraki - Lindou, Stegna 85102, Greece

Website: https://www.facebook.com/Perasma-Stegna-Rhodes-178663962173713/

6.4. Local Tavernas

Rhodes Island is home to numerous local tavernas where you can enjoy authentic Greek cuisine in a relaxed and welcoming atmosphere. These traditional establishments serve delicious homemade dishes, often prepared with fresh, locally-sourced ingredients. Here are some of the most recommended local tavernas on Rhodes Island:

1. Mavrikos Taverna Address: Eleftherias Square, Lindos 85107, Greece Website: https://www.mavrikosrestaurant.gr/

2. Kounaki Taverna Address: Kampos, Apollona 85106, Greece Website: https://www.facebook.com/kounakitaverna/

3. Ouzokafenes Address: Omirou Street 5, Rhodes Town 85100, Greece   Website: https://www.facebook.com/ouzokafenesrhodes/

4. Kastri Taverna Address: Kritinia Village, Kritinia 85106, Greece Website: https://www.facebook.com/KastriTaverna/

5. To Perasma Address: Archangelos 85102, Greece Website: https://www.facebook.com/ToPerasmaArchaggelos/

6. Ta Kardasia Address: Eleftheriou Venizelou, Afandou 85103, Greece   Website: https://www.facebook.com/takardasia.afandou/

7. To Kati Allo Address: Epar.Od. Kritinias-Embona, Embonas 85108, Greece Website: https://www.facebook.com/tokatiallo

6.5. Bars and Nightclubs

Rhodes Island is known for its vibrant nightlife, offering a wide variety of bars and lounges to enjoy a refreshing beer, a delicious cocktail, or a relaxing drink. Here are some of the best places for a drink on the island, complete with a brief description of each venue:

- **Celar of the Knights** – Platia Ippokratous, Rhodes Town. Situated in the heart of Rhodes Town, Cellar of the Knights offers a cozy and historic atmosphere, with a wide selection of local and international beverages.
- **Socratous Garden** – Sokratous 124, Rhodes Town. Nestled in a charming garden setting, Socratous Garden is the perfect spot to unwind and enjoy a refreshing cocktail or a cold beer amidst lush greenery.
- **Courtyard Bar** – Lindos; This laid-back bar in Lindos provides a unique ambiance in a picturesque courtyard setting, making it an ideal location for a relaxing evening with friends or a romantic night out.
- **Dreams Cocktail Bar** – Lindos; Dreams Cocktail Bar is known for its expertly crafted cocktails and friendly service, making it a popular destination for both locals and tourists in Lindos.
- **Lindos Ice Bar** – Krana Square, Lindos. A unique experience awaits at Lindos Ice Bar, where you can enjoy your favorite drinks in an ice-cold environment, complete with ice sculptures and a frosty atmosphere.
- **Flaws High-end Bar** – Politechniou 21, Rodos. Offering an upscale drinking experience, Flaws High-end Bar serves up premium cocktails and a sophisticated ambiance, perfect for those looking to indulge in a touch of luxury.
- **Eclipse Bar** – Lindos-Lardos Road, Pefkos. Eclipse Bar boasts a lively atmosphere and a wide selection of drinks, making it an excellent choice for a fun night out in Pefkos.
- **The Luna Bar** – Leoforos Iraklidon 92 – Ialysos. Featuring a relaxed and inviting atmosphere, The Luna Bar is the ideal spot

to enjoy a drink and some light bites while soaking in the Ialysos nightlife.

- **Captain Hook** – Orfanidou 40, Rhodes Town. A popular choice among locals and tourists alike, Captain Hook is a lively bar offering a range of beers, cocktails, and live entertainment in the heart of Rhodes Town.
- **Climax** - Ermou bar street, Faliraki. Located on the bustling Ermou bar street in Faliraki, Climax is known for its vibrant atmosphere, great music, and an extensive selection of drinks.

You can get the Online Google maps we created for you, where you can find the exact position of these bars on the map, by clicking here

6.6. Wine and Wineries

Rhodes is not only famous for its beaches and historical sites, but it is also known for its excellent wine. The island has a long tradition of wine production, dating back to ancient times. The volcanic soil and the sunny climate are ideal for growing grapes and producing high-quality wine.

If you are a wine lover, Rhodes has plenty to offer. Here are some of the best wineries to visit:

1. Emery Winery - Located in the village of Embonas, in the heart of the island, Emery Winery is one of the oldest and most renowned wineries in Rhodes. They produce a wide range of wines, including red, white, and rosé, using traditional methods and local grape varieties. Visitors can take a tour of the vineyards and the production facilities and taste some of the award-winning wines.

2. Alexandris Winery - This family-owned winery is located in the village of Salakos, in the western part of the island. They specialize in organic wines, made from local grape varieties such as Athiri, Aidani, and Mandilaria. Visitors can tour the vineyards, learn about the winemaking process, and taste some of the excellent wines.

3. Kounakis Winery - Situated in the village of Siana, on the southwestern side of the island, Kounakis Winery is another great place to taste local wines. They produce a variety of wines, including red, white, and rosé, using traditional methods and local grape

varieties such as Mandilaria, Athiri, and Assyrtiko. The winery also offers guided tours of the vineyards and the production facilities.

4. Atlantis Winery - Located in the village of Mesanagros, in the northeastern part of the island, Atlantis Winery is a small, family-owned winery that produces excellent wines using organic methods. They specialize in red wines made from local grape varieties such as Mandilaria and Mavrotragano. Visitors can tour the vineyards, learn about the winemaking process, and taste some of the unique and flavorful wines.

5. Embonas Winery Cooperative - This cooperative winery is located in the village of Embonas and is one of the largest wineries on the island. They produce a wide range of wines, including red, white, and rosé, using both local and international grape varieties. Visitors can take a tour of the production facilities, learn about the winemaking process, and taste some of the delicious wines.

6.7 Our favorite Dining Place in Rhodes

During our time in Rhodes, we sampled a variety of restaurants and cuisines, ranging from street food to high-end European and Asian fare, across various budget levels. However, one restaurant that stood out for us was "Tamam," a cozy eatery located in Rhodes town. This restaurant serves a diverse range of Greek and Mediterranean-inspired dishes in a warm and welcoming atmosphere. To top it off, they even offer complimentary mastiha liquor or ice cream to patrons. We highly recommend visiting Tamam for a truly enjoyable dining experience in Rhodes.

The food dishes that could be found only in Rhodes are:

Pitaroudia

parts of Greece. They are a simple yet delicious snack made of chickpeas, flour, onions, and various herbs and spices.

Pitaroudia are typically made by mixing the ingredients together into a thick batter and then shaping the mixture into small, flattened balls. The balls are then fried until golden brown and crispy on the outside, while still soft and fluffy on the inside. They are often served as an appetizer or snack, and are enjoyed both hot and cold.

In Rhodes, pitaroudia are often served with a side of tzatziki, a yogurt-based sauce made with garlic, cucumber, and dill. This combination of flavors and textures is both refreshing and satisfying, making pitaroudia a popular dish among locals and visitors alike.

Pitaroudia can be found in many tavernas and snack bars throughout Rhodes, especially in the Old Town area. They are typically very affordable, costing only a few euros for a serving. Some popular places to try pitaroudia in Rhodes include To Nisaki, Ta Kardasia, and Tamam, which is also known for its delicious main dishes.

If you are a fan of Mediterranean cuisine or looking to try something new, be sure to give pitaroudia a try during your visit to Rhodes.

Soupioryzo

Soupioryzo is a traditional Greek dish made with rice and a variety of vegetables, including tomatoes, onions, carrots, and celery. The name Soupioryzo is derived from two Greek words "soupia" which means cuttlefish and "ryzi" which means rice. This dish is usually made with cuttlefish, but it can also be made with squid or octopus.

To prepare Soupioryzo, the vegetables are sautéed with olive oil until they are soft and translucent. The cuttlefish or other seafood is then added to the pan and cooked until it is tender. The rice is added next and cooked with the seafood and vegetables until it has absorbed all the flavors and become soft and fluffy.

This dish is typically served as a main course and is often accompanied by a salad or other side dishes. Soupioryzo is a popular dish in many coastal towns and villages throughout Greece, particularly on the islands. It is known for its delicious and hearty flavor, and it is a great way to enjoy fresh seafood and local produce.

Lakani

Lakani is a traditional dish from the island of Rhodes, Greece. It is a type of stew made with a combination of meat, vegetables, and rice. The dish is typically cooked in a clay pot, which gives it a unique flavor and texture.

The main ingredients of Lakani usually include beef or lamb, onions, tomatoes, peppers, and carrots. The meat is first browned in oil and then mixed with the vegetables and rice. Water or broth is added to the pot and the mixture is simmered until the rice is cooked and the flavors have melded together.

Lakani is often served as a main course, accompanied by a Greek salad and crusty bread. It is a hearty and satisfying meal, perfect for a cold winter evening. It is also a popular dish for special occasions and family gatherings.

Many restaurants in Rhodes offer Lakani on their menus, but the best way to try it is to visit a local taverna or traditional Greek home.

The dish is a staple of the island's cuisine and is a must-try for anyone visiting Rhodes.

Talagkoutes – pancakes with honey and sesame

Melekouni – sesame bar with honey and slight orange taste

Don't forget to try the traditional distilled drink "Shouma," which is only produced in Rhodes. Accompany it with some local meze, such as tomato, a slice of local bread, or something salty like capers. In addition to that, you should also try classic Greek cuisine, which offers fantastic food with local vegetables, cheeses, and meats. While the menu could be extensive and cover every passion you may have, here is a list of must-try Greek dishes.

Here is a detailed guide on the top Greek dishes to try.

Greece offers fantastic food, with local vegetables, cheeses, and meat. Although the menu could be huge and cover every passion you may have, here is a list of the must-try dishes in Greece.

Try these amazing Greek Food Starters:

Tzatziki

Tzatziki is a Greek sauce that you can try with grilled meats or as a dip with bread. Tzatziki is made of strained yogurt which comes from sheep or goat milk, and it is mixed with garlic, salt, cucumbers and olive oil. You may add mint, dill or parsley. Try it with bread, fried potatoes, and grilled meat or grilled fish. And get a mint for your breath afterward

Melitzanosalata (eggplant salad).

Melitzanosalata is a traditional Greek dish made from roasted eggplants, garlic, olive oil, lemon juice, and parsley. It is a popular meze (small dish) that can be found in many tavernas throughout Greece. The dish is typically served as a dip alongside bread, crackers, or pita bread, but it can also be used as a side dish for meat or fish. Melitzanosalata is a healthy and flavorful option for vegetarians and vegans, and it is rich in antioxidants and fiber. The dish has a smoky flavor due to the roasted eggplants and a tangy taste from the garlic and lemon juice. Melitzanosalata is easy to prepare and is a perfect addition to any Mediterranean-inspired menu.

Ntolmadakia

Ntolmadakia, also known as dolmades or stuffed grape leaves, are a popular Greek appetizer. They are made by filling grape leaves with a mixture of rice, herbs, and occasionally minced meat, and then rolling them tightly into little parcels. The parcels are then boiled or steamed until the filling is cooked and the grape leaves are tender.

Ntolmadakia are typically served cold or at room temperature, and are often accompanied by a dollop of yogurt or tzatziki sauce. They can be found in most Greek restaurants and are a staple in traditional Greek cuisine.

The origins of ntolmadakia can be traced back to the Ottoman Empire, where they were known as dolma. The word dolma means "stuffed" in Turkish and refers to a wide range of stuffed dishes, including grape leaves, vegetables, and fruits. Over time, the dish spread throughout the Mediterranean and Middle East, where it took on different variations and local flavors.

Fried potatoes (Greek, French fries)

Make sure you get the fresh Greek, French fries. Some restaurants serve pre-fried ones, which are nowhere close to the original ones. Ask before you order.

Greek Salad

Greek salad, also known as Horiatiki salad, is a popular dish in Greek cuisine. It is a refreshing and healthy salad made with fresh vegetables, typically including tomatoes, cucumbers, onions, green peppers, and olives. Feta cheese is also a key ingredient in Greek salad, providing a salty and tangy flavor that complements the vegetables well.

The dressing for Greek salad is usually made with olive oil, red wine vinegar, lemon juice, garlic, salt, and pepper. Some variations may also include herbs such as oregano or basil. The dressing is drizzled over the salad just before serving, allowing the flavors to meld together.

In Greece, Greek salad is often served as a side dish or appetizer, but it can also be a light meal on its own, especially during the hot summer months. It is a nutritious and low-calorie option, packed with vitamins and antioxidants from the fresh vegetables and healthy fats from the olive oil and feta cheese.

Greek salad has become popular around the world, with many variations and adaptations to local ingredients. However, the classic combination of fresh vegetables, feta cheese, and olive oil remains a staple of Mediterranean cuisine and a favorite of salad lovers everywhere.

Spinach and cheese pie

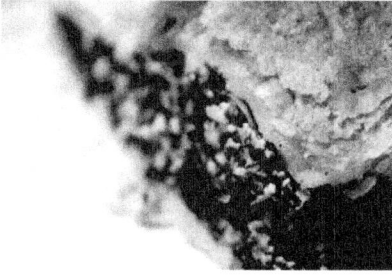

Spinach pie, also known as spanakopita, is a popular savory Greek pastry made with spinach, feta cheese, onions, eggs, and phyllo pastry. The filling is usually made by sautéing chopped spinach and onions with olive oil, then mixing it with crumbled feta cheese and beaten eggs. The mixture is then layered between sheets of phyllo pastry, which are brushed with olive oil to make them crispy and golden. The pastry is typically served as a snack, appetizer or a light meal, and it can be enjoyed hot or cold.

Cheese pie, or tiropita, is another popular Greek pastry that can be found in bakeries and cafes throughout Greece. It is made with a similar phyllo pastry as the spinach pie, but the filling is made with a mixture of feta cheese, ricotta cheese, eggs, and butter. The cheese mixture is layered between the sheets of phyllo pastry, which are then baked in the oven until they are golden and crispy. Cheese pie is often served as a breakfast or snack and can be enjoyed hot or cold.

Both spinach pie and cheese pie are popular choices for those who follow a vegetarian or Mediterranean diet. They are tasty and nutritious options, rich in protein and healthy fats. They can also be made in various sizes and shapes, such as small bite-sized pies or larger family-sized pies. Overall, these traditional Greek pastries are a delicious and convenient way to enjoy a quick and satisfying meal or snack.

Kolokithokeftedes (grilled zucchini balls)

Kolokithokeftedes, also known as zucchini fritters or patties, are a popular appetizer in Greek cuisine. These delicious fritters are made with grated zucchini mixed with onion, fresh herbs (such as dill and mint), and feta cheese, which are then formed into small patties and fried until crispy.

The name "kolokithokeftedes" comes from the Greek words "kolokithi," which means zucchini, and "keftedes," which refers to meatballs or patties. However, unlike traditional keftedes made with meat, kolokithokeftedes are a vegetarian option that is both tasty and healthy.

Zucchini fritters are commonly served as an appetizer or meze in Greece and can be found in many tavernas and restaurants. They are typically served with tzatziki sauce or a squeeze of fresh lemon juice, which adds a tangy flavor to the dish.

Kolokithokeftedes are not only delicious but also a great source of vitamins and nutrients. Zucchini is rich in antioxidants, potassium, and fiber, which are essential for maintaining good health. In addition, the feta cheese used in the recipe provides a good source of protein and calcium.

Main Courses:

Souvlaki (sticks with pork meat, grilled)

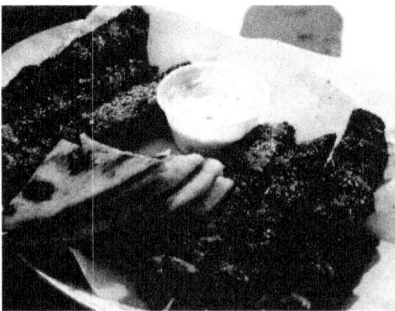

Souvlaki is a popular Greek dish made from small pieces of meat (usually pork, chicken, lamb or beef) that are skewered and grilled. The word "souvlaki" comes from the Greek word "souvla", which means skewer.

The meat is marinated with olive oil, lemon juice, herbs, and spices, giving it a delicious Mediterranean flavor. Once the meat is marinated, it is skewered and grilled over charcoal until it is cooked to perfection. The souvlaki is usually served on a plate or in a pita bread, accompanied by tomatoes, onions, and a variety of sauces such as tzatziki (a yogurt and cucumber dip), mustard, or ketchup.

Souvlaki is a popular street food in Greece and can be found at almost every taverna or grill house. It is also a staple at Greek festivals and celebrations. In addition to the traditional meat options, vegetarian souvlaki made with grilled vegetables, such as eggplant, zucchini, and peppers, is also a popular option.

Souvlaki is not only a delicious and satisfying dish but also a healthy one. The grilled meat and vegetables provide a good source of protein, vitamins, and minerals, while the use of olive oil and herbs make it a heart-healthy option. Souvlaki is a dish that truly represents the essence of Greek cuisine and is loved by locals and tourists alike.

Paidakia (lamb chops)

Paidakia is a popular dish in Greek cuisine that consists of lamb chops grilled or roasted with various herbs and spices. The dish is usually served with lemon wedges, roasted vegetables, and potatoes.

The lamb used in this dish is typically sourced from free-range or grass-fed sheep, which gives it a distinct flavor that sets it apart from other types of meat. The meat is marinated for several hours before cooking to infuse it with flavor and tenderness.

The marinade can vary depending on the region and the cook's personal preference, but it often includes ingredients such as olive oil, lemon juice, garlic, oregano, thyme, and rosemary. The lamb chops are then grilled or roasted to perfection, resulting in a juicy and flavorful meat that is crispy on the outside and tender on the inside.

Paidakia is a popular dish served at Greek tavernas and restaurants, often accompanied by a glass of red wine. It is a favorite among locals and tourists alike and is an excellent representation of the bold and hearty flavors that Greek cuisine is known for.

Moussaka

Moussaka is a popular dish in Greek cuisine that is made with layers of eggplant, potatoes, and seasoned ground beef or lamb, topped with a creamy bechamel sauce and baked until golden brown. The dish is often served as a main course and is a staple of Greek tavernas and restaurants.

The preparation of moussaka can vary depending on the region and personal preferences. Some recipes may include zucchini or other vegetables in addition to the eggplant and potatoes, while others may omit the meat or use a different type of meat.

To prepare moussaka, the eggplant and potatoes are typically sliced and fried in olive oil until they are tender and lightly browned. The meat is seasoned with herbs and spices such as oregano, cinnamon, and nutmeg, and is cooked until browned. The bechamel sauce is made with butter, flour, and milk, and is seasoned with grated nutmeg and salt.

Once all the components are prepared, the moussaka is assembled in layers in a baking dish. The bottom layer is typically the eggplant and potato slices, followed by a layer of the seasoned meat, and then another layer of eggplant and potatoes. The dish is then topped with the creamy bechamel sauce and baked in the oven until the top is golden brown and the dish is heated through.

Moussaka is a hearty and flavorful dish that is often served with a side salad or crusty bread. It is a perfect dish for a comforting family meal or for entertaining guests.

Pastitsio

Pastitsio is a popular Greek dish made with pasta, meat sauce, and a creamy béchamel sauce. It is similar to the Italian dish lasagna, but with Greek flavors and ingredients. The bottom layer is made up of tube-shaped pasta, such as penne or ziti, which is then topped with a flavorful meat sauce. The meat sauce typically includes ground beef or lamb, onions, garlic, and tomatoes, seasoned with cinnamon and other spices.

The next layer is a creamy béchamel sauce, which is made by cooking butter, flour, and milk together until it thickens. Cheese is often added to the béchamel sauce to give it extra flavor and richness. Once the béchamel sauce is ready, it is poured over the pasta and meat sauce to create a thick, creamy layer on top.

The dish is then baked in the oven until it is golden brown and bubbly. It is typically served hot, either as a main dish or as a side dish, and is often accompanied by a Greek salad and a glass of red wine. Pastitsio is a hearty, comforting dish that is popular throughout Greece, and is a favorite of many Greek families.

Fish (e.g. ask for Barbounia, Koutsomoures, which are red fried fish)

Barbounia and Koutsomoures are two popular types of fish found in Greek cuisine.

Barbounia, also known as red mullet, is a small, delicate fish with a distinctive flavor. It is typically grilled or fried and served with lemon, olive oil, and fresh herbs. In Greek cuisine, barbounia is often served whole, with the head and tail still intact. It is considered a delicacy and is often served on special occasions or as part of a festive meal.

Koutsomoures, also known as black mullet, is another popular fish in Greek cuisine. It has a firm, white flesh and a mild flavor. Koutsomoures is often grilled or fried and served with a variety of side dishes, including lemon potatoes, salad, or tzatziki. It is also a popular fish for fish soup, which is a common dish in Greek cuisine.

Both barbounia and koutsomoures are widely available in Greece and can be found on the menu of many traditional tavernas and seafood restaurants. They are often served as part of a mezze platter or as a main course. As with all seafood in Greece, they are typically served fresh and cooked simply, allowing the natural flavors of the fish to shine through.

Spaghetti with Lobster (*Astakomakaronada* in Greek)

Spaghetti with Lobster, also known as Astakomakaronada in Greek, is a luxurious and flavorful pasta dish that is popular in Greece and many Mediterranean countries. It is a seafood-based pasta dish made with fresh lobster meat, tomato sauce, garlic, white wine, and herbs like basil and parsley. The pasta used in this dish is typically spaghetti, but other long and thin pasta varieties like linguine and fettuccine can also be used.

To prepare Astakomakaronada, the lobster is first cooked in boiling water and then removed from the shell. The meat is then cut into small pieces and sautéed in olive oil with garlic and chili flakes to give the dish a bit of heat. The tomato sauce is added next, along with white wine and herbs, and simmered for a few minutes to infuse all the flavors together.

Meanwhile, the spaghetti is cooked until al dente, drained, and then added to the lobster tomato sauce mixture. The pasta is tossed in the sauce until it is fully coated and the flavors are well combined. The dish is then served hot, garnished with some fresh herbs like basil or parsley.

Astakomakaronada is a popular dish in coastal towns and islands of Greece, where fresh seafood is abundant. It is often served in upscale restaurants and is considered a delicacy due to the use of fresh lobster meat, which can be quite expensive. It is a rich and flavorful dish that is perfect for special occasions or romantic dinners.

Soutzoukakia – spiced meatballs in tomato sauce

Soutzoukakia is a popular Greek dish consisting of spiced meatballs in a rich tomato sauce. The meatballs are made of ground beef or pork, mixed with spices such as cumin, cinnamon, and garlic, and shaped into elongated, sausage-like forms. They are then cooked in a tomato sauce made with onions, garlic, tomatoes, and sometimes red wine.

The name "soutzoukakia" comes from the Turkish word "sucuk," which means sausage. The dish has Ottoman roots, as it was introduced to Greece during the Ottoman Empire's rule. However, over time, the Greeks have made this dish their own by adding their own unique twist to the recipe.

Soutzoukakia is often served with rice or potatoes, and sometimes with a side of Greek yogurt to balance out the spiciness of the dish. It is a hearty and comforting dish that is perfect for a cozy family dinner or a gathering with friends.

In Greece, soutzoukakia is a popular dish that can be found in many restaurants and tavernas. It is also a common homemade dish, with each family having their own unique recipe and way of preparing it. Soutzoukakia is a dish that has stood the test of time and remains a beloved staple of Greek cuisine.

Gemista (vegetables, usually tomatoes or pepper, stuffed with rice)

Gemista is a traditional Greek dish that features vegetables, usually tomatoes or peppers, stuffed with a flavorful mixture of rice, herbs, and sometimes ground meat. This dish is popular in the summer months when vegetables are abundant, and is often served as a main course or as part of a mezze platter.

To prepare gemista, the vegetables are first hollowed out and then filled with a mixture of rice, onion, garlic, parsley, dill, and sometimes ground beef or pork. The stuffed vegetables are then arranged in a baking dish, topped with olive oil and tomato sauce, and baked in the oven until tender and golden.

Gemista is a versatile dish and can be made with a variety of vegetables, including zucchini, eggplant, and potatoes. It can also be adapted to suit different dietary requirements, such as by using quinoa instead of rice or omitting the meat for a vegetarian or vegan version.

In Greece, gemista is often served with a side of feta cheese and crusty bread for dipping in the tomato sauce. It is a comforting and hearty dish that is perfect for sharing with family and friends, especially during the warm summer months.

Desserts you should try in Greece:

Galaktompoureko (milk pie)

Galaktompoureko, also known as milk pie, is a traditional Greek dessert made with layers of crispy phyllo pastry and a creamy custard filling. The custard is usually made with milk, sugar, semolina, cornstarch, eggs, and vanilla extract, and sometimes flavored with lemon zest.

To make galaktompoureko, the phyllo pastry is brushed with butter or olive oil and layered in a baking dish. The custard filling is then poured over the top and the dish is baked in the oven until the pastry is golden brown and crispy. Once baked, a simple syrup made with sugar, water, and lemon juice is poured over the top to add sweetness and moisture to the dessert.

Galaktompoureko is usually served cold, and can be garnished with ground cinnamon or powdered sugar. It is a popular dessert in Greece and can be found in most Greek bakeries and restaurants. The dessert is often served on special occasions, such as Easter and Christmas, but is also enjoyed year-round.

Revani

Revani is a traditional Greek dessert made of semolina flour, sugar, and eggs, drenched in a sweet syrup. It is typically served cold and garnished with chopped nuts, such as pistachios or almonds. Revani is a popular dessert in Greece and is often served at special occasions such as weddings, baptisms, and other celebrations.

To make Revani, a batter is made by combining semolina flour, sugar, eggs, milk, butter, baking powder, and vanilla extract. The batter is poured into a baking dish and baked in the oven until golden brown. While the cake is still hot, a sweet syrup made of sugar, water, lemon juice, and honey is poured over it, allowing the cake to soak up the syrup and infuse it with its sweet flavor.

Revani is a light and fluffy cake with a slightly grainy texture due to the use of semolina flour. The syrup gives the cake a sweet and tangy flavor, while the nuts provide a crunchy contrast to the soft cake. Revani can be served as a dessert after a meal or as a sweet snack with coffee or tea. It is a beloved dessert in Greece and is enjoyed by locals and visitors alike.

Halva

Halva is a sweet, dense confection made from tahini (ground sesame paste) and sugar or honey. It is a traditional dessert found in many Middle Eastern and Mediterranean cuisines, including Greek, Turkish, and Arabic. There are many variations of halva, but the basic ingredients remain the same.

To make halva, the tahini and sugar or honey are mixed together and cooked over low heat until the sugar has dissolved and the mixture has thickened. Nuts or other flavorings such as vanilla or cinnamon may be added at this stage. The mixture is then poured into a dish, smoothed out, and left to cool and set.

Halva is typically served in small slices or cubes, and can be enjoyed on its own or with tea or coffee. It is also often used as an ingredient in other desserts, such as ice cream or cake. Halva has a unique texture that is dense and crumbly, and a sweet, nutty flavor that is popular with many people. It is a great dessert option for those who are looking for a sweet treat that is not too heavy or rich.

Baklava

Baklava is a sweet pastry made of layers of filo pastry, chopped nuts (usually walnuts or pistachios), and sweet syrup or honey. It is a popular dessert in Greece, Turkey, and other parts of the Middle East and Mediterranean.

The exact origin of baklava is debated, but it is believed to have been created in the Ottoman Empire during the 15th century. Baklava is now enjoyed in various forms throughout the world, with each region putting its own spin on the recipe.

To make baklava, layers of filo pastry are brushed with melted butter or oil and then layered with a mixture of finely chopped nuts and sugar. The layers are then baked until golden brown and crispy. Once removed from the oven, the pastry is soaked in a sweet syrup or honey, allowing the flavors to blend and the pastry to absorb the moisture.

Baklava can be served in various shapes and sizes, such as large trays cut into squares or individual portions. It is often garnished with chopped nuts or a dusting of cinnamon or powdered sugar.

In Greece, baklava is commonly enjoyed during special occasions and celebrations, such as weddings and religious holidays. It is also a popular treat in cafes and pastry shops, often enjoyed with a cup of coffee or tea.

Shopping in Rhodes Island

7.1. Traditional Markets

Rhodes has a variety of traditional markets where visitors can find authentic products from the island and Greece. The most popular traditional market in Rhodes is the Municipal Market, located in the heart of the old town. Here, visitors can find fresh produce, such as fruits and vegetables, as well as local cheeses, honey, and olive oil. Other traditional markets in Rhodes include the Sunday market in Maritsa and the weekly market in Afantou.

7.2. Souvenir Shops

Rhodes has a plethora of souvenir shops that cater to visitors looking for gifts and mementos to bring back home. Some of the most popular souvenirs include local honey, olive oil, and wine. Visitors can also find handcrafted ceramics, jewelry, and textiles. The old town of Rhodes has many souvenir shops that offer unique items, such as leather sandals and hand-painted ceramics. Another popular spot for souvenir shopping is Lindos, a picturesque village with narrow streets lined with shops selling handmade jewelry and souvenirs.

7.3. Art Galleries

Rhodes is home to many talented artists, and you can find their works on display in various art galleries throughout the island. Some of the most popular ones include:

- Gallery 36: located in Rhodes Old Town, this gallery showcases a mix of contemporary and traditional art from local and international artists.

- Art Zone Gallery: situated in the heart of Rhodes town, this gallery features works of modern art from Greek and international artists.

- Ersi Gallery: located in Lindos, this gallery showcases traditional Greek art and handicrafts, including pottery, ceramics, and sculptures.

7.4. Local Products and Handicrafts

Rhodes is famous for its local products and handicrafts, which make for unique souvenirs and gifts. Some of the best places to find these include:

- The Old Town Market: located in Rhodes Old Town, this market is a hub for local artisans selling handmade ceramics, textiles, and jewelry.

- Embonas Village: located in the mountains of Rhodes, this village is famous for its local wine and honey production. You can also find handmade textiles and pottery here.

- Petaloúdes (Butterfly Valley): a nature reserve and park where you can find local herbs, spices, and handmade soaps.

7.5. Fashion and Accessories

Rhodes has a wide range of shops for fashion and accessories, from high-end boutiques to local markets. Some of the best places to shop for fashion and accessories include:

- Mandraki Harbor: a popular spot for souvenir shopping, you can find a variety of local and international brands here.

- Kolymbia: a small village located on the east coast of Rhodes, known for its designer boutiques and high-end fashion shops.

- Rhodes Old Town: the narrow streets of Rhodes Old Town are lined with shops selling handmade leather goods, jewelry, and clothing.

Outdoor Activities and Adventures

8.1. Hiking and Nature Trails

Rhodes Island offers an abundance of **outdoor activities and adventures** for all ages and fitness levels. With its stunning landscapes, lush forests, and ancient history, the island provides numerous opportunities for exploration and enjoyment.

Hiking is one of the best ways to immerse yourself in the island's natural beauty, and Rhodes has a vast network of **nature trails** to choose from. These trails cater to different levels of difficulty and take you through a variety of terrains, from coastal paths to mountainous routes.

Some of the most popular hiking trails include:

1. **The Butterfly Valley (Petaloudes)**: This picturesque trail takes you through a lush valley filled with butterflies, a unique sight especially during the summer months. The easy, well-marked path is suitable for all ages and offers an enjoyable walk through nature.

2. **Profitis Ilias** : A moderately challenging hike to the island's highest peak at 2,580 feet (785 meters). The trail starts at the village of Salakos and takes you through pine forests, offering breathtaking views of the surrounding countryside and coastlines.

3. **Seven Springs (Epta Piges)**: This relaxing walk takes you through a shaded, forested area with flowing streams and a lake. A perfect spot for a refreshing dip, the Seven Springs is a family-friendly trail suitable for all ages.

4. **Tsambika Monastery**: A short but steep hike to the hilltop monastery of Tsambika, offering panoramic views of the east coast of Rhodes. The trail begins at the Tsambika Beach and is well worth the effort for the stunning vistas.

5. **Ancient Kamiros to Kritinia Castle**: A longer and more challenging hike, this trail combines history and nature as it takes you from the ancient city of Kamiros to the medieval castle of Kritinia. Explore the archaeological site and then follow the

trail through olive groves and pine forests, enjoying magnificent views of the Aegean Sea.

Remember to always wear appropriate footwear, carry plenty of water, sunscreen, and a hat, and be mindful of the local flora and fauna. With so many incredible **hiking and nature trails** to explore, Rhodes Island is a true paradise for outdoor enthusiasts and adventure-seekers.

8.2. Watersports

Rhodes Island is renowned for its crystal-clear waters, making it a prime destination for a variety of **watersports**. Whether you're an adrenaline junkie or prefer a more leisurely pace, there's something for everyone.

1. **Windsurfing and Kitesurfing**: The island's consistent winds make it a windsurfer's paradise, especially on the west coast. Head to Prasonisi Beach, where the Aegean and Mediterranean Seas meet, to experience world-class conditions for windsurfing and kitesurfing.

2. **Scuba Diving and Snorkeling**: Rhodes offers numerous diving spots suitable for all experience levels, from beginners to advanced divers. Dive centers around the island provide courses, equipment rental, and guided dives. Explore underwater caves, reefs, and even shipwrecks teeming with marine life.

3. **Stand Up Paddleboarding (SUP)**: This popular watersport is an excellent way to explore the island's coastline and enjoy the sea. Rent a paddleboard from one of the many water sports centers and discover hidden coves and beaches.

4. **Jet Skiing and Parasailing**: For those seeking a thrill, jet skiing and parasailing are available at many popular beaches. Feel the wind in your hair as you race across the water or soar high above the shoreline for an unforgettable experience.

8.3. Boat Tours

Boat tours are a fantastic way to explore Rhodes' coastline and its surrounding islands. Numerous companies offer a range of **boat tours** to suit all interests and budgets.

1. **Sailing Excursions**: Enjoy the beauty of the Aegean Sea aboard a sailing yacht. Full-day or half-day sailing trips often include stops at secluded beaches, snorkeling opportunities, and a chance to learn basic sailing skills.

2. **Fishing Trips**: Join a local fishing boat for a unique experience, learning traditional fishing techniques and enjoying the catch of the day prepared onboard.

3. **Island Hopping**: Discover the neighboring islands of Symi, Halki, or Tilos on a day trip from Rhodes. These picturesque islands boast colorful architecture, rich history, and crystal-clear waters, perfect for a day of exploration.

4. **Sunset Cruises**: Board a boat in the late afternoon for a magical sunset cruise along Rhodes' coastline. Sip a glass of wine as the sun dips below the horizon and the sky erupts in a multitude of colors.

5. **Glass-Bottom Boat Tours**: Ideal for families, these tours provide an opportunity to observe marine life and underwater landscapes without getting wet. Marvel at the wonders of the sea while comfortably seated in a glass-bottom boat.

8.4. Scuba Diving and Snorkeling

Rhodes Island boasts a diverse underwater world, making it an ideal destination for both scuba diving and snorkeling enthusiasts. From fascinating shipwrecks to vibrant reefs, there is plenty to explore beneath the waves.

Some recommended diving centers include:

1. **Waterhoppers Diving School**: A well-established PADI 5-star Dive Resort with professional instructors, Waterhoppers offers courses for beginners as well as guided dives for certified divers. They have multiple locations around the island, including Rhodes Town and Pefkos.

2. **Lepia Dive Centre**: Based in Pefkos, Lepia Dive Centre is a PADI 5-star Instructor Development Centre offering a range of diving courses and guided dives. Their experienced team is dedicated to providing safe and enjoyable experiences for divers of all levels.

3. **Eurodivers Club**: Located in Ixia, Eurodivers Club is a PADI 5-star Dive Centre that offers a variety of diving courses, equipment rental, and guided dives. They focus on personalized service and small group experiences.

8.5. Cycling and Mountain Biking

mountain biking adventures. From leisurely coastal rides to challenging off-road trails, there are routes to suit all levels of fitness and experience.

Some recommended bike rental and tour companies include:

1. **Rhodescape**: Offering guided mountain biking tours and bike rentals, Rhodescape caters to a range of skill levels and interests. They provide high-quality bikes, safety gear, and experienced guides to ensure an unforgettable experience.

2. **Rhodes Bike Rentals**: With a wide range of rental bikes, including road bikes, e-bikes, and mountain bikes, Rhodes Bike Rentals has something for every cyclist. They also offer guided tours and suggested routes for independent explorers.

3. **Get Active Rhodes**: Specializing in guided cycling and mountain biking tours, Get Active Rhodes provides tailored experiences that showcase the island's natural beauty and cultural highlights. Their knowledgeable guides lead small groups on carefully planned routes, ensuring a memorable and enjoyable day out.

Cultural Experiences and Festivals

9.1. Museums and Galleries

Rhodes Island is home to a diverse array of museums and galleries, showcasing the island's rich history, culture, and artistic heritage. Here are some of the top museums and galleries to explore during your visit:

9.1.1. Archaeological Museum of Rhodes

Address: Plateia Mousiou, Rhodes Town Opening Hours: Tuesday-Sunday, 8:00 AM - 8:00 PM (closed on Mondays) Admission: €6 (free admission on the first Sunday of each month from November to March) Website: http://odysseus.culture.gr

Housed in a historic Knights Hospitaller building, the Archaeological Museum of Rhodes features an impressive collection of artifacts spanning various historical periods, including the Classical, Hellenistic, and Roman eras. Top exhibits include the *Marble Aphrodite Bathing* statue, the *Head of Helios*, and an array of ancient pottery, mosaics, and sculptures.

9.1.2. Modern Greek Art Museum

Address: Symi Square, Rhodes Town Opening Hours: Tuesday-Sunday, 10:00 AM - 6:00 PM (closed on Mondays) Admission: €5 (combined ticket for all three museum buildings) Website: http://www.mgam.gr

The Modern Greek Art Museum showcases a vast collection of 20th-century Greek art, including paintings, sculptures, engravings, and ceramics. The museum consists of three buildings, each dedicated to a specific art form. Highlights include works by prominent Greek artists such as Spyros Vassiliou, Yiannis Tsarouchis, and Nikos Hadjikyriakos-Ghikas.

9.1.3. Palace of the Grand Master

Address: Ippoton, Rhodes Town Opening Hours: April to October: Daily, 8:00 AM - 8:00 PM; November to March: Daily, 8:00 AM - 3:30 PM Admission: €10 Website: http://odysseus.culture.gr

The Palace of the Grand Master, also known as the Kastello, is a must-visit destination for history and art enthusiasts. Originally the residence of the Grand Master of the Knights Hospitaller, this well-preserved medieval castle now houses a museum showcasing Byzantine and medieval art, including frescoes, mosaics, and religious icons.

9.1.4. Rhodes Aquarium

Address: 28th October Str, Rhodes Town Opening Hours: Daily, 9:00 AM - 4:30 PM Admission: €5.50 (adults), €2.50 (children) Website: http://www.hcmr.gr

The Rhodes Aquarium, also known as the Hydrobiological Station of Rhodes, is a unique museum dedicated to the marine life of the Aegean Sea. Visitors can explore various aquatic exhibits, including tanks filled with colorful fish, sea turtles, and invertebrates. The museum also features an educational section showcasing preserved marine specimens and information about marine ecosystems.

Visiting these museums and galleries during your trip to Rhodes Island will provide an enriching cultural experience, offering insight into the island's fascinating history, artistic heritage, and natural beauty.

9.2. Local Festivals and Events

Rhodes Island boasts a vibrant calendar of local festivals and events, celebrating its rich history, culture, and traditions. Here are some of the top festivals and events you shouldn't miss during your visit:

9.2.1. Medieval Rose Festival

Date: Late May to early June Location: Rhodes Old Town Website: http://www.medievalfestival.gr

The Medieval Rose Festival is an annual event that transports visitors back to the time of the Knights Hospitaller. This unique festival features a range of medieval-themed activities, including street performances, music, dances, workshops, and a grand parade. It's a great opportunity to experience the island's history in a fun and immersive way.

9.2.2. Rhodes International Film Festival

Date: August Location: Various venues in Rhodes Town Website: http://www.rhodesfilmfestival.org

The Rhodes International Film Festival showcases a diverse selection of independent films from around the world, promoting cultural exchange and dialogue through cinema. Visitors can attend screenings, workshops, and panel discussions, as well as enjoy live music and other entertainment during the festival.

9.2.3. Panigiria (Saints' Day Celebrations)

Date: Various dates throughout the year Location: All across Rhodes Island

Panigiria are traditional religious festivals held in honor of patron saints throughout Rhodes Island. These vibrant celebrations typically include lively processions, music, dancing, and plenty of food and drink. Some of the most notable Panigiria include the Feast of Saint Panteleimon in July, the Assumption of the Virgin Mary in August, and the Feast of Saint Luke in October.

9.2.4. Wine and Food Festival

Date: September Location: Emponas Village Website: http://www.rhodeswinefestival.gr

The Wine and Food Festival is a gastronomic event that highlights the island's culinary heritage and local wines. Held in the picturesque village of Emponas, the festival offers visitors the chance to sample delicious local dishes, participate in wine tastings, and attend cooking demonstrations and workshops led by experienced chefs.

9.2.5. Sound and Light Show

Date: April to October, nightly Location: Palace of the Grand Master, Rhodes Town Admission: €10

The Sound and Light Show is a spectacular nightly event held at the Palace of the Grand Master, combining music, narration, and dazzling light effects to tell the story of Rhodes's history. This captivating performance is presented in multiple languages and is a memorable way to learn about the island's past.

Attending these local festivals and events during your stay on Rhodes Island will offer unique insights into the island's culture and traditions, providing unforgettable experiences and memories to cherish.

9.3. Historical Sites and Monuments

Rhodes Island is home to numerous historical sites and monuments that reflect its rich history and diverse cultural influences. Here are some of the top historical sites and monuments to explore during your visit:

9.3.1. Street of the Knights

Location: Rhodes Old Town Admission: Free

The Street of the Knights is a beautifully preserved medieval street in Rhodes Old Town, lined with impressive stone buildings that once housed the Knights Hospitaller. Strolling down this cobblestone street is like stepping back in time, as you admire the well-preserved architecture and imagine the knights who once walked these paths.

9.3.2. Monolithos Castle

Location: Monolithos Village Admission: Free

Perched atop a 300-meter-high rock, Monolithos Castle offers breathtaking views of the surrounding landscape and the Aegean Sea. Built by the Knights Hospitaller in the 15th century, the castle's ruins are accessible via a short but steep hike, making it a rewarding destination for history enthusiasts and nature lovers alike.

9.3.3. Kallithea Springs

Location: Kallithea Admission: €3 Website: http://www.kallitheasprings.com

Kallithea Springs is a stunning historical site known for its therapeutic waters and beautiful architecture. Built in the early 20th century, the site features a unique blend of Italian and Arabic architectural styles, with its elegant rotunda, lush gardens, and picturesque beach providing a serene and tranquil setting.

9.3.4. Filerimos Monastery

Location: Filerimos Hill, Ialysos Admission: €6

Filerimos Monastery is a significant religious site dating back to the Byzantine era. Situated atop Filerimos Hill, the monastery features a beautiful church dedicated to the Virgin Mary, a museum displaying religious artifacts, and a peaceful park with walking paths and peacocks roaming freely. Don't miss the impressive 18-meter-high stone cross overlooking the hill, which offers panoramic views of the island.

9.3.5. Ancient Ialysos

Location: Ialysos Village Admission: Free

Ancient Ialysos is an archaeological site showcasing the remains of one of the three ancient cities of Rhodes Island. Visitors can explore the ruins of temples, houses, and a Hellenistic stadium, providing a glimpse into the daily life of the island's inhabitants during antiquity.

Exploring these historical sites and monuments on Rhodes Island will offer a deeper understanding of the island's past and the diverse cultures that have shaped its unique identity. Don't miss the opportunity to immerse yourself in the captivating history that awaits at every corner of this enchanting island.

9.4. Music and Performing Arts

Rhodes Island boasts a lively music and performing arts scene that showcases the island's rich cultural heritage and offers visitors a chance to enjoy memorable performances in a variety of settings. Here are some of the top venues and events where you can experience Rhodes's vibrant music and performing arts:

9.4.1. Rhodes Municipal Theatre

Location: Alexandrou Diakou 2, Rhodes Town Website: http://www.rhodesmunicipaltheatre.gr

The Rhodes Municipal Theatre is a historic venue located in the heart of Rhodes Town, hosting a diverse range of events, including theatrical performances, concerts, and dance shows. With its elegant architecture and comfortable seating, the theatre offers an ideal setting for enjoying a memorable evening of entertainment during your stay on the island.

9.4.2. Medieval Rose Festival

Date: Late May - Early June (annual) Location: Rhodes Old Town Website: http://www.medievalrose.org

The Medieval Rose Festival is an annual event that takes place in Rhodes Old Town, celebrating the island's medieval history and traditions. The festival features a variety of performances, including music, dance, and theater, as well as workshops, exhibitions, and reenactments, providing an immersive experience of the island's rich cultural past.

9.4.3. Rhodes International Jazz Festival

Date: September (annual) Location: Various venues across Rhodes Island Website: http://www.rhodesjazzfest.com

The Rhodes International Jazz Festival is a highly anticipated event that showcases local and international jazz talent in a series of concerts and performances held at various venues across the island. The festival aims to promote jazz music and culture on Rhodes Island, offering a unique opportunity to enjoy world-class performances in picturesque settings.

9.4.4. Sound and Light Show at the Palace of the Grand Master

Location: Palace of the Grand Master, Rhodes Old Town Admission: €10

During the summer months, the Palace of the Grand Master hosts a spectacular sound and light show that takes visitors on a journey through the island's history. The show features stunning visual effects and an engaging narrative, providing a captivating experience for audiences of all ages.

9.4.5. Orpheus Open-Air Cinema

Location: Ippoton 9, Rhodes Old Town Website: http://www.orpheus-cinema.gr

For a unique cinema experience under the stars, visit the Orpheus Open-Air Cinema in Rhodes Old Town. This charming venue offers a selection of international films and Greek classics, screened in their original language with Greek subtitles. Enjoy a relaxing evening of entertainment in the cinema's cozy garden setting, complete with a bar and snacks.

Rhodes Island's music and performing arts scene caters to diverse tastes and interests, providing visitors with ample opportunities to experience the island's rich cultural heritage and enjoy unforgettable performances in a range of enchanting venues.

Tips for Travelers

10.1. Health and Safety

Rhodes Island is generally a safe destination, but it's important to take basic precautions and be prepared for potential health and safety concerns during your travels:

1. **Travel Insurance**: Make sure your travel insurance covers any activities you plan to participate in, such as watersports or hiking. Ensure it includes medical expenses, personal liability, trip cancellations, and lost or stolen belongings.

2. **Documentation**: Carry a copy of your passport, travel insurance, and other essential documents in case of loss or theft. Keep digital copies accessible on your phone or in your email for added security.

3. **Sun Protection**: Protect yourself from the sun by wearing sunscreen with a high SPF, sunglasses, and a hat, especially during the hottest parts of the day.

4. **Hydration**: Stay hydrated by drinking plenty of water, particularly when engaging in physical activities or spending time in the sun.

5. **Pharmacies**: Pharmacies on Rhodes Island are well-stocked with over-the-counter medications and basic first-aid supplies. Be aware that they may have limited hours, especially in smaller villages. If you require prescription medications, bring an adequate supply and a copy of your prescription with you.

6. **Hospitals and Medical Centers**: In case of a medical emergency, Rhodes has several hospitals and medical centers, including Rhodes General Hospital (located in Rhodes Town), private clinics, and smaller health centers in various towns and villages. Keep a list of the nearest medical facilities to your accommodation.

7. **Emergency Numbers**: Familiarize yourself with local emergency numbers. The general emergency number in Greece is 112. For specific services, you can call the following numbers:

- Police: 100

- Ambulance: 166

- Fire Brigade: 199

8. **Embassies and Consulates**: Know the location and contact information for your country's embassy or consulate in Greece. In case of legal issues or emergencies, they can provide assistance and guidance. Note that some countries may not have an embassy or consulate on Rhodes Island itself, but in Athens or other major cities in Greece.

10.2. Currency and Money Exchange

The official currency in Greece is the Euro (€). It is advisable to have some cash on hand, particularly for small purchases, as not all businesses accept credit cards. You can exchange money at banks, post offices, or authorized currency exchange offices. ATMs are widely available in Rhodes, especially in larger towns and tourist areas.

1. Avoid exchanging money at airports or hotels, as their rates are usually less favorable.

2. Keep an eye on exchange rates to get the best deal, and be aware of any fees associated with currency exchange.

3. Inform your bank of your travel plans to avoid any issues with your credit or debit card while abroad.

10.3. Tipping Etiquette

Tipping is customary in Greece, although not obligatory. Here are some general guidelines for tipping on Rhodes Island:

1. In restaurants, a tip of 5-10% is appreciated for good service, but check your bill to see if a service charge has already been included.

2. For taxi drivers, rounding up the fare or adding 5-10% is a common practice.

3. Hotel staff, such as porters or housekeepers, may appreciate a small tip of 1-2€ for their service.

4. It is not necessary to tip in bars or cafes, but you can round up your bill or leave the change if you wish.

5. When participating in guided tours or activities, it is customary to tip the guide 5-10€, depending on the quality of the experience and the duration of the tour.

Remember, tipping is a personal choice and should be based on the quality of service you receive. Be considerate and show your appreciation for good service while enjoying your time on Rhodes Island.

10.4. Language and Communication

The official language of Rhodes Island is Greek, but due to its popularity as a tourist destination, English is widely spoken in most areas, especially in hotels, restaurants, and tourist attractions. Nevertheless, learning a few basic Greek phrases can greatly enhance your travel experience and help you connect with locals:

1. Καλημέρα (Kaliméra) - Good morning

2. Καλησπέρα (Kalispera) - Good evening

3. Ευχαριστώ (Efcharistó) - Thank you

4. Παρακαλώ (Parakaló) - Please / You're welcome

5. Συγγνώμη (Sygnómi) - Excuse me / Sorry

6. Ναι (Né) - Yes

7. Όχι (Ochi) - No

To facilitate communication, consider downloading a Greek language app or carrying a pocket-sized phrasebook. Most Greeks appreciate the effort made by visitors to learn their language and are likely to be more helpful and friendly when approached with a few Greek words.

10.5 Practical Tips and Information

- **Book Flights and Accommodations**: To secure a reasonably priced room and affordable flights, make your reservations well in advance. The peak season runs from early April to the end of October.

- **Local Tourist Information**: Visit the Dodecanese Islands' tourist office in Rhodes city, situated at the corner of Makariou & Papagou St., adjacent to the New Market.

- **Exploring Rhodes Town**: Rhodes Town is best explored on foot; wear comfortable shoes for easy walking.

- **Swimming Months**: The optimal months for swimming are July, August, and September. June and October are generally suitable, although the sea is cooler than in peak months. The western side can be windy with rocky beaches, while the best beaches are on the eastern side.

- **Navigating Unnamed Roads**: Many small towns and villages have unnamed roads. Don't hesitate to ask for directions if you need help finding your way!

- **Parking in Rhodes Town**: Parking can be challenging in Rhodes Town. Check here for parking lots.

- **Souvenirs to Bring Back Home:** Local craft jewelry, Umbrellas, Wine, Olive oil, Olive wood bowls, Local honey, Loukoumi and melekouni sweets, Hand-woven carpets and sponges

- Time zone in Greece is **UTC +2**.

- The island's highest point is Mount Attavyros (1219m) and there lies an ancient temple dedicated to Zeus.

- Rhodes has a Mediterranean climate with hot -and often humid- summers and mild, moist winters. July and August are usually the hottest months. Rhodes has an average of 300 days of sunshine a year! For more on Rhodes' climate check out the weather station here

- Banks: Open from Monday to Friday 08.00-14.00pm. You can find a list of banks in Rhodes here ATMs are everywhere.

- Credit Cards: Internationally recognized credit cards are accepted at restaurants, shops, and hotels.

- **Best place to drink a morning coffee:** Koukos; drop by here in the morning to drink a coffee and grab some delicacies for your breakfast.

- **Best Ice-cream:** Stani.

- **Best Traditional Greek food restaurants:** Steno and Poloniatissa

Steno Restaurant: you need a reservation here. It has tables in a beautiful yard, very good prices and tasty food. You have to park well before arriving here.

Steno Restaurant Menu

- **Best Seafood Restaurant:** Perigiali and Gialos restaurants, both at Stegna area which worths a visit on its own to see the dramatic landscape with the rocks and the sea.

A view of the mountains at Stegna area Stegna area - a panoramic view

Gialos restaurant in Rhodes Gialos restaurant - outside view

Gialos restaurant - inside view

Gialos is famous for the spaghetti with shrimps or seafood (32 euros for two persons).

We suggest trying the seafood kritharoto for two people (27 euros), ladopita, and potato salad. The salty fish, however, may not be to everyone's taste. The crowd here is generally young and local, with Greek music playing in the background. Occasionally, someone may break into a zeimpekiko dance. To finish off your meal, you'll be treated to ice cream and baklava.

Best Souvlaki: Bahar and then **Stavlos**. Both are great value for money, and excellent places to try gyros, souvlaki and grilled chicken. They are meat only.

Stavlos has always a line of people waiting to be seated as it has a few tables outside, on the pavement.

We liked Bahar even more. Try the Roditiki ladopita with gyros or souvlaki.

TOP 3 places to watch the sunset in Rhodes:

You can enjoy the sunset at one of these sites. Their position is highlighted on the map, at the end of this guide.

- Monte Smith, Rhodes Town

-Psaropoula, Rhodes Town

- The west-side hotel's roof gardens (consider Amathus or Sheraton in Ialysos)

Suggested Itineraries

11.1. 3-Day Rhodes Island Getaway

Day 1: Exploring Rhodes Town

08:00 - 09:00: Start your day with breakfast at your accommodation or at a local café.

09:00 - 11:00: Visit the **Palace of the Grand Master of the Knights of Rhodes**. This stunning medieval castle houses a museum and offers beautiful views of Rhodes Town. Entrance fee: €6.

11:00 - 13:00: Stroll along the **Street of the Knights** and explore the well-preserved medieval buildings, ending at the **Archaeological Museum of Rhodes**. Entrance fee: €6.

13:00 - 14:30: Have lunch at a local taverna, such as **Ta Kardasia**, offering traditional Greek dishes.

14:30 - 16:30: Wander around the **Old Town of Rhodes**, a UNESCO World Heritage site, and visit the **Suleiman Mosque** and **Roloi Clock Tower**. Entrance fee for the tower: €5.

16:30 - 18:00: Take a break and enjoy a Greek coffee or an iced frappé at **Kastri Café**.

18:00 - 20:00: Walk along the **Mandraki Harbour** and visit the **Fort of St. Nicholas** for panoramic views.

20:00 - 22:00: Enjoy dinner at **To Kanoni** restaurant, specializing in Greek seafood dishes.

22:00 - 23:00: End your day with a leisurely stroll along the waterfront before heading back to your accommodation.

Day 2: Exploring Lindos and the East Coast

Note: Rent a car for this day to maximize your time and flexibility.

08:00 - 09:00: Have breakfast at your accommodation or a local café.

09:00 - 10:30: Drive to **Lindos** (approximately 50 km from Rhodes Town).

10:30 - 13:00: Explore the **Acropolis of Lindos,** a magnificent archaeological site with stunning views. Entrance fee: €12.

13:00 - 14:30: Have lunch at **Mavrikos** in Lindos, a family-run restaurant offering delicious Greek cuisine.

14:30 - 16:30: Relax and swim at the picturesque **St. Paul's Bay**.

16:30 - 18:00: Drive north along the east coast, stopping at **Tsambika Beach** for a refreshing swim.

18:00 - 20:00: Continue to **Seven Springs (Epta Piges)**, a beautiful nature reserve with walking trails and a small lake.

20:00 - 21:30: Drive back to Rhodes Town and have dinner at **Kerasma Restaurant** for traditional Greek dishes and live music.

21:30 - 23:00: Enjoy a leisurely walk around Rhodes Town and return to your accommodation.

Day 3: Exploring the West Coast and Valley of the Butterflies

Note: Keep the rental car for this day as well.

08:00 - 09:00: Start your day with breakfast at your accommodation or a local café.

09:00 - 10:00: Drive to the **Valley of the Butterflies (Petaloudes)**, a lush nature reserve famous for its seasonal butterfly population (June to September). Entrance fee: €5.

10:00 - 12:00: Explore the valley's walking trails, taking in the beautiful surroundings and observing the butterflies.

12:00 - 13:30: Drive to the village of **Embonas** and have lunch at **Kounaki Taverna,** known for its homemade Greek dishes and local wines.

13:30 - 15:00: Visit **Kritinia Castle** on the west coast, a 16th-century Venetian fortress offering stunning views of the coastline. Entrance fee: Free.

15:00 - 16:30: Head to **Fourni Beach** for a relaxing swim and sunbathing session.

16:30 - 18:30: Continue to the **Ancient Kamiros** archaeological site, an impressive ancient city with well-preserved ruins. Entrance fee: €4.

18:30 - 20:00: Drive back towards Rhodes Town, stopping at the **Monolithos Castle** for breathtaking sunset views. Entrance fee: Free.

20:00 - 21:30: Return to Rhodes Town and have dinner at **Tamam Restaurant** for a fusion of Greek and Middle Eastern cuisine.

21:30 - 23:00: End your 3-day Rhodes Island getaway with a leisurely stroll around Rhodes Town, enjoying the nighttime ambiance before returning to your accommodation.

11.2 3-Day Rhodes Island Classics with Details and Maps

1st Day In Rhodes - Itinerary

09:00: Arrival at Rhodes "Diagoras" International Airport, located 15 km west of Rhodes Town.

09:30: Take the bus to the city center or a taxi directly to your hotel. Check-in and settle into your room. Cost: €2.2 (bus), around €25 (taxi)

10:30: Head to the archaeological site on **Monte Smith Hill** to visit the **Acropolis of Rhodes**. The Acropolis features sanctuaries, temples dedicated to Apollo, Athena, and Artemis, public buildings, a library, and a stadium. This open-air site is always open and offers stunning views of the town. Cost: Free

13:00: Lunch at **Tamam Restaurant** Address: Leontos 1, Rhodes Town, Tel: +30 2241073522

14:00: Visit the **Archaeological Museum of Rhodes**. Housed in a building that was once the Knights' Hospital, the museum's exhibitions take visitors through the island's history from prehistoric to Hellenistic times. Cost: €8 (ask for the special package or check the museum's website for eligibility in reduced entrance)

15:30: Explore the **Palace of the Grand Master of the Knights** and wander around the **Medieval City**.

18:00: Head to **Elli Beach**. This famous beach offers a cosmopolitan atmosphere and is one of the most visited spots on the island. Enjoy the clear waters, sunbathing, and people-watching. Elli Beach has a rich history that leaves one's imagination to wander, especially considering that English writer Lawrence Durrell once described it as the finest beach in the Mediterranean. The vibrant multi-colored umbrellas, sunbathers from around the world relaxing on sunbeds, impressive hotels, and notable landmarks like the Casino and the Aquarium, once the focus of many photographers, now grace the front of nostalgic postcards. Each day, Elli Beach attracts countless international visitors and locals alike, who come to enjoy a refreshing break by the sea.

19:30: Have dinner at **Taverna Thomas**. Address: Leontos 8, Rhodes Town, Tel: +30 2241073557

21:00: Discover Rhodes Town by night. Take a leisurely stroll and enjoy the vibrant nightlife. For a beer or a cocktail, we recommend visiting the **Cellar of Knights** pub.

1st Day in Rhodes - Map

Below you can get the maps that correspond to all the activities that we recommend for your first day in Rhodes. These maps are accessible on Google Maps so that you can quickly zoom in/out and use them from your tablet or smartphone when you are in Rhodes.

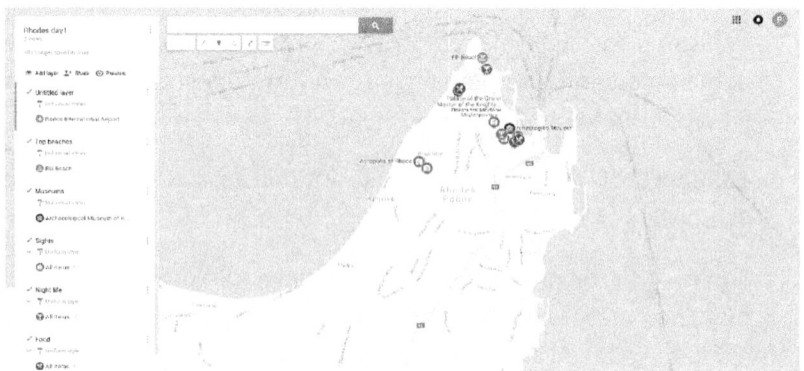

Click here to view the map online.

Acropolis of Rhodes

The Acropolis of Rhodes is an acropolis dating from the Classical Greek period (5th–3rd century BC) 3 kilometers from the center of Rhodes.

The partially reconstructed part of the site consists of the "Temple of Apollo" (also, as alternatives Athena Polias and Zeus Polieus) below which is a stadium and a small theater. It is included in a large park, Monte Smith, named for English Napoleonic Admiral William Sidney Smith.

History

The island of Rhodes is the largest of the Dodecanese, an island group in the southeastern Aegean Sea. In 408 BC, near the end of the Peloponnesian War, three of the island's ancient cities merged to build an entirely new one - the city of Rhodes - on a site in the Ialysia region of the island. Admired for its beauty and luxury, the city flourished.

After weathering a siege by Demetrios Poliorketes (the Besieger) in 305-303 BC, Rhodes rallied and built the Colossus of Rhodes, a massive statue of the sun god Helios, to whom Rhodes is linked in

Greek mythology. The Colossus is known as one of the Seven Wonders of the Ancient World. Following the great earthquake in 227 BC, which toppled the enormous harbor statue and devastated the city, Rhodes was rebuilt. Cassius later raided it in 42 BC and never recovered. Another catastrophic earthquake in AD 515 caused Rhodes to be reduced and confined to the area of Palais Polis, the present-day Old Town. Over the next centuries, it was raided by the Persians and the Arabs, and after holding off the Ottoman Empire in 1480, Rhodes was conquered by the Turks in 1522. In their war with the Turks, the Italians occupied the Dodecanese islands in 1912, which were not liberated until 1945, at the end of World War II. At that time the British oversaw the islands until their eventual incorporation into Greece 1948. Most recently, Rhodes (the island) has become a popular holiday destination for tourists.

Excavation and Restoration

The original excavation was carried on by the Italian School of Archaeology at Athens from 1912-1945. Following World War II, the Greek Archaeological Service took over excavation and restoration of the ruins. This included extensive reconstruction of the Temple Pythian Apollo, which was extensively damaged by bombing and artillery installed there during the war. Excavation began in 1946, and continues today in the Acropolis archaeological park, which covers 12,500 square meters, and is protected from any new construction.

Site

The Acropolis is situated on the highest part of the city. The monuments were built on stepped terraces, with solid retaining walls.

Temple of Athena Polias and Zeus Polieus

Located at the northern extreme of the Acropolis in an east-west orientation, this stately temple was dominated by Doric columned porticos on all sides and formerly housed the written treaties the Rhodians held with other states. A stoa bounded the temple to the east.

Nymphaeums

Just southeast of the Temple of Athena Polias and Zeus Polieus are four subterranean "structures" cut into the rock, featuring entrance steps, passages, and a large opening in the central roof, along with water cisterns, foliage, and interior niches for statuettes. These "caves" were used for worship and recreational purposes.

Temple of Pythian Apollo

Smaller than the Temple of Athena Polias and Zeus Polieus, this structure boasts a similar east-west orientation but is located on the southern end, just west of a large rectangular terrace. Part of the northeast side of this porous peripteral temple has been restored.

Odeon

This small marble theater held approximately 800 spectators. Situated northwest of the Stadium, it is believed to have been used for musical performances and rhetoric lessons of prominent Rhodians.

Stoa Building

The impressive façade was visible from even the harbor. Today just one foundation wall remains.

Artemision

The Artemis cult's place of worship is situated on the northeast side of the hill, amidst the ruins of other structures of similar function.

Stadium

Located on the southeast side of the hill, the 210-metre north-south Stadium was initially restored by the Italians. It is surviving features include the sphendone (rounded end with turning post), proedries (officials' seats), and some of the spectator seating. The starting apparatus used in the athletic events has also been preserved. Athletic events of the Haleion Games, honoring Helios, were held here.

Click here to visit the: Website

Archaeological Museum

The Archaeological Museum of Rhodes is a museum located in the Medieval City of Rhodes. The Museum contains various collections of archaeological artifacts from the Isle of Rhodes.

Click here to Visit the: Website

Palace of the Grand Master of the Knights

The Palace of the Grand Master of the Knights of Rhodes, also known as the Castello, is a medieval castle in the city of Rhodes, on the island of Rhodes in Greece. It is one of the few examples of Gothic architecture in Greece. The site was previously a citadel of the

Knights Hospitaller that functioned as a palace, headquarters, and fortress.

History

The palace was originally built in the late 7th century as a Byzantine citadel. After the Knights Hospitaller occupied Rhodes and some other Greek islands (such as Kalymnos and Kastellorizo) in 1309, they converted the fortress into their administrative center and the palace of their Grand Master. In the first quarter of the 14th century, they repaired the castle and made some significant modifications. The castle was damaged in the earthquake of 1481, and it was restored soon afterward.

After the Ottoman Empire had captured the island, the palace was used as a command center and fortress. The lower part of the castle was severely damaged by an ammunition explosion in 1856. As a result, many rooms on the first floor were destroyed.

During the Italian rule of Rhodes, the Italian architect Vittorio Mesturino restored the damaged parts of the palace between 1937 and 1940. It became a holiday residence for the King of Italy, Victor Emmanuel III, and later for Fascist dictator Benito Mussolini, whose name can still be seen on a large plaque near the entrance.

On 10 February 1947, the Treaty of Peace with Italy, one of the Paris Peace Treaties, determined that the recently established Italian Republic would transfer the Dodecanese Islands to Greece. In 1948, Rhodes and the rest of the Dodecanese were moved as previously agreed. The palace was then converted into a museum and is today visited by the millions of tourists that visit Rhodes.

In 1988, when Greece held the rotating presidency of the European Economic Community (as the European Union was known back then), Greek Prime Minister Andreas Papandreou and the other leaders of the EEC had a traditional party in the Palace.

Address: Ippoton, Rodos 851 00, Phone: 2241 365270

Built: 7th century, 14th century

Click here to visit the: website

Medieval Town

The Order of St John of Jerusalem occupied Rhodes from 1309 to 1523 and set about transforming the city into a stronghold. It subsequently came under the Turkish and Italian rule. With the Palace of the Grand Masters, the Great Hospital and the Street of the Knights, the Upper Town is one of the most beautiful urban ensembles of the Gothic period. In the Lower Town, Gothic architecture coexists with mosques, public baths and other buildings dating from the Ottoman period.

The citadel of Rhodes, built by the Hospitallers, is one of the best-preserved medieval towns in Europe, which in 1988 was designated as a UNESCO World Heritage Site. The city of Rhodes is a popular international tourist destination.

Website

Elli beach

Being one of the most famous Greek beaches among photographers, the beach of Rhodes still offers something of its cosmopolitan aspect from the 70's and is one of the most visited beaches on the island. Hundreds of tourists and locals visit the beach daily.

2nd Day In Rhodes - Itinerary

08:30: Visit **Lindos Acropolis and Ancient Theater**. The Acropolis of Lindos offers a unique blend of architectural and historical elements from various periods, including ancient Greek temples, Hellenistic buildings, Roman temples, the Knights' castle built over Byzantine fortifications, and a Greek Orthodox church. Cost: (Check official website for current prices) View ZoomTip 2.2

11:00: Relax at **Agios Pavlos (Saint Paul) Beach**. See Top 10 beaches in Rhodes.

13:30: Lunch at **Mythos Restaurant**. Address: Lindos Tel: +30 22440 31300 Email: info@MythosLindos.com

14:30: On your way back to Rhodes, stop at one (or more!) of the stunning beaches between Lindos and Rhodes Town (Haraki, Agathi, Stegna, Afantou, Traganou, Antony Quinn Bay, or Kallithea Springs). View Top 10 beaches in Rhodes and Zoom Tip 2.1

18:30: Enjoy an evening walk around Rhodes Town. Discover landmarks like the Medieval Clock, Nea Agora (New Market), Fort of Saint Nicholas, and Mandraki Harbor (the alleged location of the famous Colossus statue).

20:00: Have dinner at **Kathopoulis Family Restaurant** and return to your hotel. Address: Themistokleous 5-7, Rhodes Tel: +30 2241 026707

For those who want to continue their evening out, Rhodes offers numerous pubs and bars in the town and nearby villages. Our recommendations include:

- Climax (in Faliraki)

- Luna Bar (in Ialysos)

- Captain Hook (in Rhodes Town)

- Flaws High-end Bar (Rhodes Town)

- Captain Hook (Rhodes Town)

2nd Day in Rhodes – Map

Below you can get the maps that correspond to all the activities that we recommend for your second day in Rhodes. These maps are accessible in Google Maps format so that you can quickly zoom in/out, navigate and use them from your tablet or smartphone when you are in Rhodes.

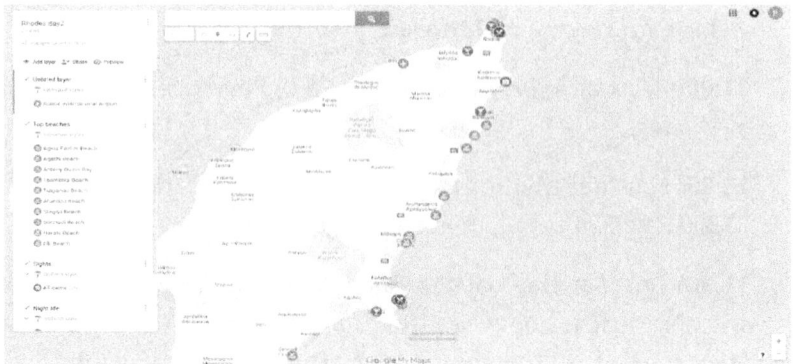

Click here to view the map online.

The Acropolis of Lindos

Lindos, is an archaeological site, a town and a former municipality on the island of Rhodes, in the Dodecanese, Greece. Since the 2011 local government reform, it is part of the municipality Rhodes, of which it is a municipal unit. The municipal unit has an area of 178.900 km2.[3] It lies on the east coast of the island. It is about 50 km south of the town of Rhodes, and its fine beaches make it a popular tourist and holiday destination. Lindos is situated in a large bay and faces the fishing village and small resort of Charaki.

Above the modern town rises the acropolis of Lindos, a natural citadel which was fortified successively by the Greeks, the Romans, the Byzantines, the Knights of St John and the Ottomans. This makes the site difficult to excavate and interpret archaeologically. The Acropolis offers spectacular views of the surrounding harbors and coastline.

On the acropolis of Lindos today parts of the following buildings may still be seen:

- The Doric Temple of Athena Lindia, dating from about 300 BC, built on the site of an earlier temple. Inside the temple are the table of offerings and the base of the cult statue of Athena.

- The Propylaea of the Sanctuary, also dating from the 4th century BC. A monumental staircase leads to a D-shaped stoa and a wall with five door openings.
- The Hellenistic Stoa with lateral projecting wings, dating from about 200 BC. The stoa was 87 meters long and consisted of 42 columns.
- The well-known relief of a Rhodian trireme (warship) cut into the rock at the foot of the steps leading to the acropolis. On the bow stood a statue of General Hagesander, the work of the sculptor Pythokritos. The relief dates from about 180 BC.
- The Hellenistic staircase (2nd century BC) leading to the main archaeological area of the acropolis.
- Remains of a Roman temple, possibly dedicated to Emperor Diocletian and dating from about 300 AD.
- The Acropolis is surrounded by a Hellenistic wall contemporary with the Propylaea and the stairway leading to the entrance to the site. A Roman inscription says that the wall and square towers were repaired at the expense of P Aelius Hagetor, the priest of Athena in the 2nd century AD.
- The Castle of the Knights of St John built some time before 1317 on the foundations of older Byzantine fortifications. The walls and towers follow the natural conformation of the cliff. A pentagonal tower on the south side commanded the harbor, the settlement and the road from the south of the island. There was a large round tower on the east facing the sea and two more, one round and the other on a corner, on the northeast side of the enceinte. Today one of the towers at the southwest corner and one to the west survive.
- The Greek Orthodox Church of St John, dating from the 13th or 14th century and built on the ruins of a previous church, which may have been built as early as the 6th century.
- Some scenes of the well-known film, The Guns of Navarone, were filmed here.

Click Here to Visit the: Website

The Ancient Theater of Lindos

Website

Medieval clock

Nea Agora (Newmarket)

Fort of St. Nicholas

Mandraki Harbour

The Mandraki, was the military harbor and was guarded by a tower built between 1464 and 1467 by the Grand Master Zacosta at the end of the natural mole. After the siege of Rhodes in 1480, the Grand Master d'Aubusson added a bastion around the tower transforming it into a guarded fortress on the sea.

3d Day in Rhodes – Itinerary

08:30: Check out from the hotel and visit the **Bee Museum**. This unique museum in Greece showcases the island's rich beekeeping tradition. Learn about the life of bees, the beekeeping process, and taste local products. Don't forget to purchase honey or "melekouni" sweets as a souvenir! View ZoomTip 3.1

10:30: Swimming time at one of the **Top 10 Beaches**. See Top 10 beaches in Rhodes.

13:00: Lunch at **Anthoula Tavern** in Kolympia. Address: Kolympia Tel: +30 2241 056205

14:00: Visit **Tsambika Church** and spend your last hours on the island at **Tsambika Beach**. Tsambika is a small Byzantine church dedicated to Holy Mary. According to the legend, women who struggled to conceive would climb there barefoot to pray. The name Tsambika is unique to Rhodes. Climbing the hill offers stunning, panoramic views of the coastline. Cost: Free View ZoomTip 3.1

17:00: Head to Rhodes (Diagoras) Airport for your departure. View ZoomTip 2.3

3d Day in Rhodes – Map

Below you can get the maps that correspond to all the activities that we recommend for your third day in Rhodes. These maps are accessible on Google Maps so that you can quickly zoom in/out and use them from your tablet or smartphone when you are in Rhodes.

Get this map online by clicking here

ZoomTip 3.1: Information on the Monuments

Bee Museum

Visit the one-of-a-kind **Bee Museum** in Greece and immerse yourself in the fascinating world of bees through transparent observation hives. Discover the tradition and history of beekeeping in Rhodes, and learn how honey is obtained from the bees to our tables.

Gain in-depth knowledge about bees and their valuable products, including honey, pollen, wax, propolis, and royal jelly. Stroll through the bees' garden and become familiar with the Rhodian herbs and flowers that attract these industrious insects.

Don't miss the opportunity to taste and purchase all-natural bee products at the museum's on-site store.

Bee Museum

Website: http://www.mel.gr/en/content.asp?id=4

Address: Epar.Od. Kalithies-Pastidas, Rodos 851 06, Greece, Hours: Open today · 8:30am–5pm, Phone: +30 2241 048200

Tsambika church

This is a monastery on top of a hill which offers a great view, if you are brave enough to climb the 305 steps. You will hear moving stories about the miracles that took place here, especially for mothers who were trying to have children. It's a good place to spend some time on the way to Lindos. Probably, it offers the best view on the island.

Tsambika beach

Tsambika is an 800 meters long beach of fine pure sand, gently shelving on the east coast of the island of Rhodes. Distant at about 26 km from the capital, this pure-sand beach has survived from permanent development as most of the land is owned by the Orthodox Church. In fact, at the north end of the beach, on a sharp peak overlooking the beach, there is the church of Panagià Tsambika.

This beach is considered as one of the best beaches on the island. It has crystal clear waters and it's considered ideal for families with children as it is all sandy and shallow. There are umbrellas and loungers, watersports and a few canteens for sandwiches, ice cream and refreshments.

Tsambika can be reached by public transport but it is better to get there by car or bike as there are a lot of interesting surroundings to explore.

Rhodes offers a wide variety of daily excursions and activities to make your trip even more enjoyable. Here are some recommended options:

Symi Island Excursion

A visit to the picturesque island of Symi is a must when staying in Rhodes. Just a short boat trip away, Symi is known for its beautiful neoclassical architecture, colorful houses, and crystal-clear turquoise waters. Spend the day exploring the island's main town, Gialos, and its charming harbor, or venture up to the hilltop village of Chorio for stunning panoramic views. Don't forget to visit the iconic Panormitis Monastery, dedicated to Archangel Michael and renowned for its impressive frescoes and peaceful atmosphere.

To make the most of your day in Symi, consider joining a guided tour or booking a boat excursion. Many tour operators in Rhodes offer day trips to Symi, which usually include transportation, a knowledgeable guide, and ample time for sightseeing, swimming, and enjoying local cuisine.

Kos Island Excursion

Another great day trip option from Rhodes is the nearby island of Kos. Known for its rich history, beautiful beaches, and lively atmosphere, Kos offers a delightful combination of relaxation and exploration.

Begin your day by visiting the ancient Asklepieion, an important healing temple and medical center dedicated to the god of medicine, Asclepius. Then, explore Kos Town's historic landmarks, including the Castle of the Knights, the Ancient Agora, and the Roman Odeon. Stroll through the picturesque streets of the town, admiring the charming architecture, and don't miss the chance to visit the famous Tree of Hippocrates, where the renowned physician is believed to have taught his students.

After exploring the island's cultural and historical attractions, unwind on one of Kos's beautiful beaches, such as Tigaki, Kardamena, or

Paradise Beach. These sandy shores offer crystal-clear waters, ideal for swimming and sunbathing.

To make the most of your day on Kos, consider joining a guided tour or booking a boat excursion. Many tour operators in Rhodes offer day trips to Kos, which usually include transportation, a knowledgeable guide, and ample time for sightseeing, swimming, and sampling local cuisine.

Marmaris Excursion

For a unique day trip experience from Rhodes, consider visiting Marmaris, a bustling resort town on the Turkish coast. With its beautiful beaches, historic sites, and lively atmosphere, Marmaris offers an enjoyable mix of relaxation and exploration.

Start your day by visiting Marmaris Castle, which dates back to the 16th century and now houses a museum showcasing the area's history and artifacts. From the castle, enjoy panoramic views of Marmaris and its picturesque marina.

After exploring the castle, wander through the Marmaris Old Town, admiring the charming streets lined with traditional houses and shops. Visit the bustling Marmaris Bazaar, where you can shop for souvenirs, spices, clothing, and authentic Turkish goods. Don't miss the opportunity to try some delicious local food at one of the many restaurants in the area.

For a relaxing afternoon, unwind on one of Marmaris's beautiful beaches, such as Icmeler Beach or Turunc Beach. These sandy shores offer crystal-clear waters, ideal for swimming and sunbathing.

To make the most of your day in Marmaris, consider joining a guided tour or booking a boat excursion. Many tour operators in Rhodes offer day trips to Marmaris, which usually include transportation, a knowledgeable guide, and ample time for sightseeing, swimming, and enjoying local cuisine. Keep in mind that you will need a valid passport and may need a visa to enter Turkey, so plan accordingly.

Halki Excursion

For a peaceful and relaxing day trip from Rhodes, consider visiting Halki, a small and picturesque island in the Dodecanese. Known for its tranquility, crystal-clear waters, and traditional architecture, Halki is an ideal destination for those looking to escape the crowds and immerse themselves in authentic Greek island life.

Begin your day by exploring the charming harbor town of Emborio (also known as Nimborio), the island's main settlement. Wander through the narrow streets and admire the colorful neoclassical houses, many of which date back to the 19th century. Don't miss the opportunity to visit the Church of Agios Nikolaos, which boasts a beautiful bell tower and frescoes.

For a taste of Halki's history, take a hike or rent a bike to visit the abandoned village of Chorio, located uphill from Emborio. Here, you'll find the ruins of medieval houses and the 14th-century Castle of the Knights of St. John. From the castle, enjoy stunning panoramic views of the island and the Aegean Sea.

Halki's pristine beaches are perfect for swimming, sunbathing, and snorkeling. Visit popular spots like Pondamos Beach, Ftenagia Beach, or Kania Beach, and take a dip in the crystal-clear waters. For a more secluded experience, consider renting a boat or joining an organized boat tour to discover hidden coves and less accessible beaches around the island.

To make the most of your day in Halki, consider booking a guided tour from Rhodes, which usually includes transportation, a knowledgeable guide, and time for sightseeing and beach hopping. Alternatively, you can take the ferry from Rhodes to Halki independently and explore the island at your own pace.

Rhodes Map

The map below includes every point of interest mentioned in this guide. Furthermore, includes some museums and other extra sights which you may want to visit if you have some more time or in case you want to alter our recommended itinerary.

Click here to view it on Google maps

Thank You

As you conclude your journey through Rhodes and its neighboring islands, you'll undoubtedly leave with a treasure trove of memories and experiences that will last a lifetime. From the awe-inspiring history and well-preserved medieval architecture of Rhodes Town to the stunning beaches and charming villages scattered throughout the region, this Greek island paradise offers something for every traveler.

We hope this travel guide has provided you with valuable insights and inspiration for your trip, but remember that there is always more to discover. Embrace the spirit of adventure, venture off the beaten path, and immerse yourself in the local culture. Talk to the locals, try the traditional cuisine, and soak up the unique atmosphere that makes this corner of the Mediterranean so special.

As you return home, don't forget to share your experiences with friends and family, and encourage them to explore Rhodes and its neighboring islands for themselves. The beauty, history, and warmth of this enchanting region will surely continue to capture the hearts of those who visit, just as it has captured yours.

Safe travels, and we hope to see you again soon in Rhodes and the Dodecanese Islands!

Your friends at Guidora.

most web publishers, our current view is that acceptance of the 'Non Commercial' condition means (1) we must not sell the image or any publication containing the image (2) we may, however, use an image as an illustration for some information which is not being sold or offered for sale.

Note to other copyright owners

We are grateful to those copyright owners who have given permission for their material to be used. Some of the material comes from secondary and tertiary sources. In every case, we have tried to locate the original author or photographer and make the appropriate acknowledgment. In some cases, the sources have proved obscure, and we have been unable to track them down. In these cases, we would like to hear from the copyright owners and will be pleased to acknowledge them in future editions or remove the material.

Printed in Great Britain
by Amazon